Praise for A

"*And So Somehow* is a story of the power of faith in our world as lived by a woman whose very beginning, and her life thereafter, is a testimony to that power. The story is an account of Joy's mission to serve the Lord by battling one of the darkest evils in this world—human sex trafficking—and the cost to her life, her soul and her beliefs as she hurled the gauntlet down again and again."

—MICHAEL J. FERJAK, B.S., M.A. 40-year Veteran Law Enforcement Investigator, International Trainer and recognized Human Trafficking Expert, *I Know A Guy* Training & Consulting, LLC

"What an encouragement! *And So Somehow* is much more than a memoir. She takes you by the hand and invites you to walk with her through her journey to a new life. In the process, you gain the tools to move from ashes to resurrection life yourself. It is one of the most insightful books I have ever read. I highly recommend this book!"

—TERRY BAXTER, Cofounder of GoServ Global

"Joy is a woman who skillfully writes her own story of God's redeeming grace from a difficult life of abuse and lack of self-worth. *And So Somehow* offers hope to hurting people by inviting them to experience a personal relationship with Jesus Christ that will change their lives. God will use this book to bring healing and hope to those who need it the most."

—PAUL VAN GORKOM, Executive Director, GoServ Global, Inc.

"Joy Fopma's life is a tapestry of deep faithfulness, forgiveness and healing. It is clear her heart's desire is for every reader to see Jesus' pursuit, through redemptive love and resurrection power, as the common thread woven throughout her own life and His pursuit for the reader's heart as well. This powerful book of raw honesty is a gift laced with the consistent hope we have in Jesus."

—JULIE VAN HOVE, Founder, Defined Ministries

"This is a book you won't be able to put down. Joy's story is all of our stories because we all experience suffering in some form growing up in this fallen world. The words on these pages dance with hope as the threads of the heartache of suffering are woven together with the hope of resurrection life . . . not waiting for eternity but within one's grasp now. This book reveals a beautiful tapestry of what a yielded life in the Master's hands can become when the choice is made to go through the journey of healing rather than trying to avoid or deny it. Get ready to discover a path to your own "resurrection" within the pages of this life-transforming book!"

—KATHIE HOBSON, National Training Director and Facilitator of *The Ultimate Journey*

"Joy's life and testimony are a beautiful illustration of the *And So Somehow* miraculous work of God. Her love for Him and others is illuminated in this powerful message of hope. Even more than the "how to," she shares the 'One who truly brings about the how!'"

—LISA HUBERS, Prayer Ministry Director, Omega Life Christian Ministries

"Joy walks into the prison of her past and, step by step, shares transparently how she is led through the fire of fear, to the Truth that unlocks the door and sets her free. Walk with her as she shares her journey of redemption and you'll suddenly realize: *And So Somehow* resurrection is happening in you!"

—KARYN BRINKMEYER, Executive Director, Omega Life Christian Ministries

"The power of this incredible story is its realness. It is filled with brokenness and beauty, told with candor and vulnerability, reading it filled my eyes with tears and my heart with hope. It made me want to be the hands of Jesus extended to others."

—DR. RICHARD BOATMAN, Pastor, Oakwood United Methodist Church

"*And So Somehow*, what a telling title. God never ceases to amaze me with how he takes our worst nightmares and makes a love story out of it. And Joy's story is just that. I have known Joy since 2015, when I joined the work of survivor care for sexually exploited women. In many ways, she was my mentor and is loved dearly. The work she has done in this field has touched many. This book will give you hope and allow you to fall in love with Jesus. Grab a cup of coffee, tissues, and this book if you want to see a great God make beauty out of ashes ... somehow!"

—BRENDA LONG, Founder and Executive Director, Garden Gate Ranch

"Joy Fopma does an amazing job of telling her story. Whether it was the hurt from her family of origin, her own failures, or the pain of divorce, woven through her story are the amazing ways Jesus held her and brought her through. This is a resource I will use often to encourage clients who will easily connect with the gut wrenching pain and ultimate victory she so graciously writes about."

—TRUDY M. JOHNSON, PhD., LMFT, CCTS-1, Executive Director and Founder of Anesis Retreats

"*And So Somehow* captured my attention within the first pages. I read it in its entirety with few breaks. Tears blurred the words as God's deep wound healing resonated into the tender parts of my own heart. Tears of compassion rolled freely to know her pain but Joy doesn't leave her readers in the valley of sorrow. You will feel hope arise. This riveting account of Joy's life will lead many through their own path of healing."

—M. KIM COMBES, M.Ed., Director of Combes Counseling and Consultation and From Pain to Passion International, Author of *Walk in a Manner Worthy: A Voice in the Foster & Adoptive Care Wilderness*

"*And So Somehow* is a deeply moving journey of resilience and faith. Joy's raw and honest storytelling captures the essence of a life transformed by grace and the power of testimony. This book is not only a beacon of hope for those who have faced struggles but also a testament to the strength found in vulnerability and the pursuit of healing. Her courage to share her story will undoubtedly encourage others to step into their own light."

—ANDREW ALLEN, President & CEO of Youth Shentler Services of Iowa, '95 YSS Alumnus

"My family and I love Joy and have known her and her family for a long time. She is an excellent transparent communicator. She will point you to the Lord who heals as she takes you into her journey of saying yes to receiving Jesus, surrendering to Him through suffering, and so somehow, to walk in resurrection as an overcomer!"

—PASTOR RICK SUMMER HAYES

"Joy's desire for others to experience the *and so, somehow resurrection* on this side of eternity is beautifully expressed in her memoir: you can almost hear her exclaiming, "Freedom is possible for you! Come find it with me!" Joy invites you to tag along as she embarks on a personal journey of embracing the mess of her humanity as she experiences the collision of death and resurrection that points to her true identity in Christ. Along the way, you find yourself examining your own heart and how the Creator of it speaks to you."

—KELLY BUTCHER, Development Coordinator, Wings of Refuge

"This truly is a story of beauty from ashes! Joy speaks candidly through her personal story about deep hurts that are, sadly, far from uncommon. If you've ever wondered where God is or if you're too far gone, you need to read this. If you have ever prayed a prayer like Joy did: 'God, if you are real I need to know it. I need you to show me. I need you to come and save me. Come and save me from myself.' Hurting and broken sister, come along and find a friend; you are not alone!"

—ANGEL ARMSTRONG, SonScape Retreats, Program Director | Retreat Leader

"Infused with raw vulnerability and hard-won wisdom, this courageous and moving memoir penetrated my very soul. Joy's gift of writing (Mrs. Thompson was right!) transcends the reader into her story, allowing them to feel a part of her pain and triumph. Like dawn gifting light to a dark night, so does God bring a welcome and essential light into the dark recesses of her life. Thank you, Joy, for giving words to *And So Somehow*, and for sharing it with a wounded world, desperate for the hope you found."

—TERESA DAVIDSON, ARNP, MSN, MA, | CEO, Chains Interrupted

"Being invited to walk the rooms of another person's life is sacred. Joy is generous with her story and vulnerability. She reflects brightly her God and accurately the hard, but good, journey life is when we follow him. This book weaves Joy's story, with God's and the stories of women. It is so important for us to hear. You won't be sorry you picked this book up."

—STEPHANIE PAGE, Executive Director, Stories Foundation

"I have been encouraged by Joy's story for years and am thankful for her faithfulness in following where the Lord has led and what He has asked of her. As a woman impacted by her witness, I know, love, and continue to pursue Christ in my life. I pray And So Somehow blesses you as it has me."

—RACHEL H., "You spoke at my church, and you saved my life" Story on page 126-127

And So Somehow

And So Somehow

My Story of Finding Joy
in Suffering
and Resurrection

JOY FOPMA

Copyright © 2024 by Joy Fopma

Cover Design: Heidi Caperton

All rights reserved. No part of this book may be reproduced or transmitted in any form or by any means, electronic or mechanical, including photocopying, recording or by any information storage and retrieval system, without permission in writing from the copyright owner. For information on distribution rights, royalties, derivative works or licensing opportunities on behalf of this content or work, please contact the publisher at the address below.

Instances where a bible translation was not listed, NIV was likely used.

Scripture quotations marked (NIV) are taken from The Holy Bible, New International Version® NIV®. Copyright © 1973, 1978, 1984, 2011 by Biblica, Inc.® Used by permission of Zondervan. All rights reserved worldwide.

Scripture quotations marked (AMP) are taken from the Amplified® Bible, Copyright© 1954, 1958, 1962, 1964, 1965, 1987 by the Lockman Foundation Used by Permission. (www.Lockman.org)

Scripture quotations marked (NLT) are taken from the Holy Bible, New Living Translation. Copyright ©1996, 2004, 2015 by Tyndale House Foundation. Used by permission of Tyndale House Publishers, Carol Stream, Illinois 60188. All rights reserved.

Scripture quotations marked (TPT) are taken from The Passion Translation®. Copyright © 2017, 2018, 2020 by Passion & Fire Ministries, Inc. Used by permission. All rights reserved. ThePassionTranslation.com.

Although the author and publisher have made every effort to ensure that the information and advice in this book were correct and accurate at press time, the author and publisher do not assume and hereby disclaim any liability to any party for any loss, damage, or disruption caused from acting upon the information in this book or by errors or omissions, whether such errors or omissions result from negligence, accident, or any other cause.

Printed in the United States of America.

This book is dedicated to:

Family

Acknowledgments

I want to thank my family and friends for who they are and for their gracious support and encouragement. I also want to acknowledge every person who is part of my story. I pray my words bring honor to all . . . those I mention and those I do not. This story continues as God weaves His golden thread of resurrection through the high points, low points, and all the boring Tuesdays in between.

Table of Contents

Acknowledgments . . . . *xiii*
Foreword . . . . *xvii*
Prologue . . . . *xix*
Chapter 1: The Moments That Made Me 1
Chapter 2: Tangled-up Innocence 9
Chapter 3: Little Girl Lost. 17
Chapter 4: My Double Life 27
Chapter 5: A Normal Life 35
Chapter 6: March 5, 2007 43
Chapter 7: Write the Pain 53
Chapter 8: Me? A Princess. 59
Chapter 9: Two Steps Forward, One Step Back 65
Chapter 10: Mission and Purpose 73
Chapter 11: Forward and Back Again 79
Chapter 12: Miracles in Africa. 89
Chapter 13: A Formal Invitation Into Suffering 99
Chapter 14: The Other Side of the Door. 107
Chapter 15: The Hostage. 115
Chapter 16: On a Mission 121
Chapter 17: And So Somehow. 133
Chapter 18: And They Lived. 139
Chapter 19: Life Goes On 145

Chapter 20: Dancing Again 153

Afterword: And So Somehow: A Practical Guide *157*

About the Author. *169*

Foreword

*She lives fully convinced that God is able
to do whatever He promises.*

—Romans 4:21 NLT (paraphrased)

And So Somehow is a story of brokenness and loss: a story of shattered dreams and disappointments. At the same time, it is also a story of redemption, hope, and promises fulfilled. It lives in the tension of good and evil, of lies and truth, of a hurt, broken, little girl and a fiercely passionate, brave woman.

Readers will weep with the hurting little girl and cheer for the brave woman as Jesus replaces the innocence lost with His resurrection power. Joy is literally and figuratively restored to a life of restoration and freedom. Those who have heard her speak are blessed. Those who read this book will be inspired. Those who know her as a friend and fellow sister-in-Christ understand she is a gift straight from Heaven.

And So Somehow shines light in the darkness of suffering. That light is Jesus. It illustrates beautifully that somehow in the fellowship of His suffering, we find something that we cannot find anywhere else: His nearness; His compassion; His deep, Fatherly love. He is the Wounded Healer. He is the Light.

His resurrection power is free to all who will receive. Acceptance of this free, life-changing gift transforms lives. It transformed Joy's. It transformed mine. Once you experience His freedom, like Joy, hopefully you too will be compelled to go tell people about the Light because life on earth is short. What you do with Jesus Christ will determine where you will spend eternity. Let's spend it together in Heaven!

And so somehow ... God Wins!

—BEV SHIPLEY, Former Director of Wings of Refuge

Prologue

Some stories are more difficult to write than others. Mine is one of those stories. Finding the words and the purpose were sometimes very difficult for me; the memories of my past paralyzed my thoughts at times and motivated my fingers at other times. One particular winter, when I was feeling very stuck and praying for guidance, God answered in the most beautiful and unexpected way. He used my son, Trey, as His messenger to speak into my heart. For my Christmas gift, Trey wrote and gave me the following essay. The gift was priceless, and I will be forever thankful for it. It was exactly what I needed to finish my book.

WRITE

by Trey Foose

Tap … Tap … Tap … There she sat; thoughts swirling around her head as fragments of the story started to resurface. She swore the screen never looked so full of ideas. Whether it was scripture or chicken-scratch, the words began to appear. There was no stopping her. The page was her canvas, a conduit to another realm where she was instructed to place the stars for the very first time. Click . . . Clack . . . The sounds of angels singing as her life began to pour out onto the page. Click . . . Clack . . . She not only wrote of herself but her children, her parents. The celestial family tree made it evident that her thoughts were not rooted in narcissism or self-glory but rather alluded to the roots from which she sprang. Clickity . . . Clackity . . . Typos were corrected like ink spilling back into the pen. She is amazed by the ingenuity, not made but given to her from The Grand Creator.

Tap . . . Tap . . . Tap . . . There she sat; thoughts began to torment her as she could only hit one key: the backspace. Chaos and deceit entered the story, as she wondered if some stars were black holes in disguise, swallowing up truth. The canvas was too abstract, and the themes became obstructed. The chants of critics' voices within changed the story on her. Whether it was gospel or heresy, she continued to write. A slave to her ambition she battled what needed to be shared and what needed to remain with her. She now saw her twinkling stars as demerits of judgment and uncertainty. Click . . . Clack . . . Days flew by as no new pages sprawled out. The process of revision led to a decline within her initial intent of the document. A scattered masterpiece that she called a mess, and an unwritten biography that was her life. Click . . . Clack . . . The focus came back as she revisited her favorite writings, verses, and passages. The thoughts began to streamline as she found a new purpose. The constant questioning being answered in the paragraphs yet to come, and the stanzas yet to be written. Clickity . . . Clackity . . . Her one reader, a secret admirer that wrote the thoughts before she could even put it into words. And, so, she was able to write.

Tap . . . Tap . . . Tap . . . There she sat; knelt before the unjust station of the writer's block. Wondering how she found herself back here after days of productivity. She had tried everything to stay in the flow of emotion and clarity of the story, but she

PROLOGUE

couldn't foresee the drought. She prepared for this, or so she had thought. With many of the pages complete, she struggled, wondering if this was only the beginning. No amount of coffee or free time could unfreeze her. There she sat . . . Click . . . Clack . . . Yes, the same sound, but not made by her. She dropped to the floor, sobbing. The one who penned the story before she even came to be showed her the reason to write. She saw her reader thirsty for hope. Click . . . Clack . . . She received the greatest love-letter ever written. She began to speak the words she could not put to page, not as advice or a cautionary tale, she began to ask if she was ready to accept the great burden of the Author. Clickity . . . Clackity . . . The Spirit filled the room as she cried and lifted her eyes to fix upon The One and only truth that mattered. The truth of an author that dared to write, not for Himself, but specifically, for her. At once, she knew the truth is not hard to believe when it is written for you. Bread and wine secured her words; Faith affirmed her story. *And So Somehow . . .* She wrote.

Chapter 1

The Moments That Made Me

*Before I formed you in the womb I knew you,
before you were born I set you apart*
—Jeremiah 1:5 NIV

The thief comes only to steal and kill and destroy. I came that they may have life and have it abundantly.
—John 10:10 NIV

It was a steamy August afternoon, the kind where the cliched phrase of *"It's not the heat, it's the humidity,"* was indulgently overused. A young couple met for a casual dinner with friends in the hope of passing the time as they eagerly awaited the birth of their first born child.

The unexpected pains of contractions interrupted the dinner conversation early on. Even though the due date was weeks away, a trip to the hospital overtook the evening agenda. The scene changed from a casual dinner with sweat and picnic flies to a sterile hospital room with bright lights and medical staff.

"Push! Push! Push and do not stop! Push! Do not stop pushing!"

Panic hung heavy in the air, stronger than a barometric pressure that makes the bones ache as the doctor passionately coached the mother to be. Crisis medical equipment was ushered into the room. Doctors and nurses maneuvered quickly about. The young mother pushed and pushed with all her might, yet it was not enough. There was a delivery but it was not a baby. Nurses scurried about, unhesitatingly following the strict orders that were spoken in stressed tones under the doctor's breath. A father sat outside, unaware that life and death hung in the balance of his newly forming family. The placenta that had sustained life inside the womb over the past nine months, forged in front of the baby's delivery and now campaigned for death.

The inexperienced mother could feel the weight in the room but she had no point of reference to know if this was normal or not. Tension was thick. Time stood still. The physician pulled the baby into the world by forceps as protocol had taught him. Silence screamed where the joyous cry of a baby should have been. An ocean of anxiety flooded the room like a tidal wave. The staff tread in the monstrous waters calmly performing all the processes they had been taught sitting in an orderly classroom to prepare them for this moment. Could anything have prepared them for this moment? Their hearts sank to their toes. They continued to work on the baby. I wonder if their minds shouted, "Please cry, baby, so your mama doesn't have to."

And then it happened. In what seemed like a frozen eternity, a first cry melted the silence. The announcement of new life filled the air. An aura of relief washed over everyone and the room which now resembled a war zone. I caught my breath for the first time as squeals gained their volume and protruded out of my fresh little lungs.

Many times mom told the story of my birth and how she didn't know at the time the miracle that it was. "Most babies delivered after the placenta are stillborn." her doctor explained. She simply knew that in that moment she met the "joy" of her life. And so she named me just that.

From my first breath, Divine and darkness were in the room, a foreshadowing of what was to come.

Innocent beginnings of faith marked my life. Before I could speak, the name of Jesus was spoken over me. I was prayed over until I learned to pray my own *Now I lay me down to sleep, I pray the Lord my soul to keep,* and sung to until I sang *Jesus Loves Me This I know.* Sunday school, bible school, and church camp were commonplace. Debuting as an angel in the Christmas pageant at the First Baptist Church was a dream come true. Our family rarely missed church on any given Sunday and routinely, with all the other little Baptist girls, I was properly clothed in twirly dresses with big bows at the waist and matching black patent Mary Janes for Christmas and Easter.

The wonders of God delighted me. One Christmas Eve night, while lying quietly in bed attempting to settle my excited heart, I saw a vision of heavenly hosts in my mind's eye, a vast difference from the expected visions of sugar plums dancing in little heads. The purest tones of crystal clear angelic sounds filled me with joyful peace as I slumbered in their worship. When I woke to the anticipated Christmas morning and gleefully told my mom, "I heard the angels sing," she was terrified, thinking hearing the angels meant I may be dying. I, on the other hand, was elated and can still recall the angelic sounds in my heart that once lulled me to sleep.

The mystery of God enchanted my innocent heart. I desired to sing like the angels and float on clouds. I clearly remember my bare toes wandering about our front yard as summer's agenda presented another clear schedule for the day. Something stirred in my heart. I carefully picked a preschool-sized fist of bright yellow dandelions. One by one I formed my bouquet. Chubby fists now full, I smiled into the big blue sky. Sunbeams streamed through the crisp clouds and warmed my face. The moment warmed my soul. I knew there was a big God up there. I breathed deep, closed my eyes, and began twirling. Without thought, I swayed freely. Little made-up love songs to that faraway good man in the sky began flowing out of me. I sang quietly with my whole heart as I twirled about the green dance floor. My only audience was a few oak trees standing at attention. I proudly lifted the golden hand-picked treasure clenched inside my little hands, and offered it as a gift to that great big God above the sun.

Do not despise these small beginnings, for the Lord rejoices to see the work begin, to see the plumb line in hand.

—Zechariah 4:10 NLT

The day of dandelions and dancing marked the mustard seed plumb line of faith growing in little me. I believed in something I could not see: the cumulus clouds and the God who made them seemed reachable. I was in awe and wished for time to stand still. A feeling of being known and knowing filled me.

Dreams floated in my young mind of one day being on a stage and speaking about this great big God up there. He saw me. I mattered. My little heart desired more.

I wish I could tell you my life was one dandelion dance after another. Sometimes it was.

Warm fuzzy experiences of childhood are treasures stored away in my mind from camping with my family: eating, gooey toasted marshmallows around the campfire, and fishing with my dad.

Waking up with the sun streaming through my bedroom window as birds melodically chirped to welcome a day, running through sprinklers, eating too many red popsicles, and riding my banana seat bike with my sister and neighborhood friends are common memories when I look back.

We were a family who did not fly or travel much, so the one flight we did take to Texas to visit my aunt and uncle terrified me. I begged to get off the plane, squirming vigorously to break free and bolt before the cabin door shut. My dad firmly held me, hot and red faced with tears, while he sang, *One glad morning when this life is over, I'll fly away.* His singing calmed me and I felt safe in his arms.

Mom loved to cook midwestern comfort food for family and friends. Her table was open and many often gathered there. My homemade-by-mom Hollie Hobbie birthday cake, (yes, I was born in the 70's; Google it, young ones!) made me so proud, I was hesitant to blow out the candles on it. It was certainly too pretty to eat!

Lori, my younger sister by 21 months, seemed more like my twin. She was my best friend along with our neighbor Missy. Our little girl gang, the JLM Cub, which besides our initials also doubled for Jesus loves me, held concerts in the backyard to raise money for Africa, singing the hit 80's song *We are the World*, and went "on tour" singing about Jesus to all the nursing homes in our small town with coordinated outfits and memorized choreography. We were tiny visionaries who filled the neighborhood with entrepreneurial feats selling Grandpa's fresh-picked garden produce in our red wagon as we went door to door, and established a members-only *Official Ricky Schroder Fan Club*.

Josh, my baby brother was the miracle Jesus gave to us: a great surprise. God spoke to mom and told her she was going to have a little boy and to name him Joshua. I couldn't wait to be a really big sister. Having a baby brother and being 10 would be like being a little mama with a real live doll. I thought I had hit the jackpot until my little brother was born too early. He was premature and got an infection in his blood stream when the umbilical cord was cut. The doctor told my parents he might not make it. Besides my own entrance into the world I had not had the threat of death come to someone so close. I was sad and scared. I didn't understand what was happening—except Mom was gone and I wanted her home. A lot of people were praying and bringing food to our house, and grandma was staying to take care of us because Dad worked and went to the hospital. But mostly mom knew it was just a good idea to have Grandma there. The days dragged on. Joshua fought for his life while the tubes and IVs coming out of him did the same.

One night, exhausted and feeling helpless to help her premature little boy who was losing weight while an infection rampaged through his blood stream, Mom prayed, "Lord, He is yours. Thank you for giving me this little boy, but I give him back to you." Mom surrendered in that moment and knew that no matter what God would take care of her son. The next morning the doctor came in and shockingly explained to mom that the tests were showing that the infection was responding to the treatments. Jesus healed that little peanut and he came home! He was the best thing ever —a real live doll that my sister and I doted on and fought over.

My mind is full of happy times with grandparents who loved Jesus and valued family. Christmas at Grandma and Grandpa's was packed full of people, a mountain of presents, and wonderful smells coming from the kitchen while we opened gifts. Holiday gatherings filled with faith, food, family and friends: laughter and togetherness. It sometimes seemed as if I lived inside a nice family sitcom whose problems were solved in a 30-minute window every week.

I am often amazed at how God allows us to remember such wonderful moments. Memories are a movie inside us with feelings and thoughts that come to life each time you rewind and hit play on them. When a fresh pack of spearmint gum is opened, its scent mingles with leather. I am taken to Grandma's purse sitting in the pew of the First Baptist Church magically supplied with fresh packs of gum for me each Sunday. She gives me the look and I give her a smile as she moves like an undercover agent seamlessly gliding her hand inside her bag, slides it out and places her hand in mine with the concealed silver package. Touching that tender place causes a smile and a tear from those moments even now. I believe that God, in his kindness and mercy, lets us experience and remember such moments because he knows we'll need them. He knows our minds will need something precious and sweet to hold on to when the storms of life come.

My innocent beginnings are a part of who I am. The high points of holy moments and happy times made me. Golden threads of faith and gospel were woven into little me. A tapestry of love began to form me, yet it was a far cry from perfect. The majority of my youth would not be found on any highlight reel. The twisted and tangled threads of chaos on the backside of a tapestry feel like a better description of my childhood when I look back.

Chapter 2

Tangled-up Innocence

"How did we get here?" I wondered as my mind drifted from the precious parts of my childhood and back to the present as I sat on the edge of the stiff hospital mattress and held the hand of the one who birthed mine. It wasn't my first time sitting in Heaven's birthing room with someone I loved. The signs were evident, Mom's words were becoming few and her gaze far off. Rest was the work preparing her to move into eternity.

Swirling thoughts drove inside my head like bumper cars as I watched my mom prepare to die. My soul wanted to yell "Cut!" like a movie director as I thought about all the life lived between my first breath, and her impending last. "Can we please have a do-over?"

There was no do-over. We were here. It had all happened and it was happening. Life was slipping through my fingers like sand and all the granules of my life with my mom on earth were almost through my fingers. I wanted to scoop up another pile, place it in my palm and begin again. How could it be that my mother felt like a stranger?

AND SO SOMEHOW

The Storm Inside Our Walls

My Father's temper was the heat that sparks wild storms: the kind of heat that makes you sweat when you're sitting still. Sticky heat on summer afternoons that turns fun under the sun into furiously finding shelter. There was no radar to know the weather in our home, only sirens declaring the tornado had touched down. Real or perceived happenings hit his emotional reactor that made his hand instinctively rip off his belt and begin his path of destruction. When my tiny arm caught his path it was game over. The cyclone smack of his belt flopped incessantly in the raging windstorm hitting my bare skin over and over and over.

"This is hurting me more than it will ever hurt you!" The wind of him howled in a wild laugh that increased in volume with every word.

Lighter thunderstorms rumbled that varied from smacks across my face or across my heart.

A looming cloud of loathing hung over my father at every duration of a common cold or 24-hour flu. "Call Fosters!" (our local funeral home) "I'm not going to make it!" he begged and pleaded through moans like a broken record. When mom said "Stop," he turned into an uncontrollable crying little boy who wailed and whimpered.

Sometimes he was a sad, pitiful rain cloud. The evening spaghetti accidentally slid off his plate and onto our new carpet; he flew out of control and threw his plate like a frisbee, watered the spaghetti with his glass of fresh sun tea, pitched the glass like a baseball, and stomped out of the house cursing and screaming with threats that we would never see him again. I sat eating my spaghetti terrified and relieved; the storm was over for now but when would it stir back up again? If it was gone forever how would we survive? Every Friday we met him for lunch at the factory and he gave mom the paycheck that bought our groceries and kept our lights on.

When my father wasn't a tornado, he was a leaky faucet that annoyingly dripped with boisterous teasing, pestering, and provoking. This was my father's M.O. (mode of operating). A finger in my ears, ribs, or belly, at my neck, flicking my nose, or forced hugs that I could not get out of were unwelcome rituals. I skirted from him, hid behind my mom, or voiced, "Please stop!"

"What's wrong with you? I was just teasing you. I was just loving you, don't you want to be loved? Don't you love me? I guess nobody loves me."

I instinctively pulled away while mutually feeling sorry for him: the one nobody loved.

What he labeled play, I labeled terror. It was common to be pinned to the ground under his protruding belly while he tickled me until I went into a hysterical fit. The sick joy he got from my screams made my tiny mind shout, "Help!" inside.

My father hid and popped out at unsuspecting times, usually behind my bedroom or bathroom door after I had showered or used the bathroom. It was so normal that eventually, I was not scared by it at all. As a little girl, I thought all of this was completely normal and was what dads did.

My best strategy was to stay out of his path of destruction the best I knew how. If he had excess food to stuff himself, a radio to tinker with, and time alone in his garage, I knew the possibility of a good night was in my favor. If the tornado alarm sounded, my best option was to run to my closet and bury myself under clothes to escape his unpredictable rage. Just as the warmth of Grandma's love washes over me when I smell spearmint, my breath feels heavy and my body feels frozen as I remember the stale scent of smelly shoes and clothes that needed washing while staying completely still, holding my breath until I thought I would faint; hoping to disappear under the pile of clothes and arrive back into the dandelion dance once again.

"I bet you can't make this one, I bet you're gonna miss!" was his sideline lingo as I shot hoops in the driveway. When I missed, he shouted with glee, "Ha, I told you that you couldn't do it! You're no good!"

"I can do this. Try again. Yes! I made it. I can! Did you see that, Dad?" my mind chanted back.

"Lucky! That was luck! Bet you can't do it again," he mocked. A strong will rallied me to battle and prove him wrong. Passion cheered as I picked up the ball and tried again until his non-stop ridicule filled me with defeat.

"Why are you stopping? Are you a quitter? I was just teasing you. Can't I tease you?" Victory was his alone. Self-hatred seeds were planted in the soil of my heart and began to grow like weeds. How do I stop this? What was so bad about me? What had I done to earn the rejection of my father? Would anything ever change?

Smile and Look Pretty

Mom's answer to the chaos was, "Smile and look pretty." A trophy shelf of awards could have filled our home for the performances of this system we acted out through the unpredictable narrative of my father. Even with red puffy eyes and a tear-stained face, I could swallow emotions and tap into "smile and look pretty" for Mom. I pretended and performed in order to survive. On the inside I was wading through quicksand, never knowing when a sinkhole of the unpredictable chaos would pop open and attempt to swallow me up. From the outside I portrayed that *everything was just fine.*

The "Smile and look pretty" mask fooled others so I could please mom. I tried hard to be pretty and perfect while learning how to run faster and faster on a performance-based treadmill through life. Pretty clothes, perfectly styled hair, minding my manners, and having a smile in front of others no matter what I truly felt usually kept the peace. Near-perfect grades, trying hard to not make messes, keeping the house immaculately clean, and staying out of her way were ways mom would be momentarily happy. When she was happy, I was proud. It kept me going to think maybe one day Mom and Dad would be happy: like the neighbors whose father was a banker. He wore a suit and a smile every day. He was clean, calm, and put together. On the occasions I played there, he came home from work smiling with a kiss for his wife. They had a snack drawer, but it didn't seem to bring them happiness like ours did. Maybe if I was good enough our family could one day be: Just. Like. That.

I tried my best to please mom and make her happy. It was impossible. I was a little girl with vision, passion, and an imagination; who made messes, had big emotions, and a very strong will. I came to believe the jingle my mother often quoted me: "There was a little girl who had a little curl right in the middle of her forehead. When she was good, she was very, very good, but when she was bad, she was horrid." I believed I was a very horrid little girl, but did my best to be a very, very good little girl. No matter what I did or how hard I tried, the same result played out: Mom was not happy and therefore I was horrid.

I smiled while anxiety overwhelmed me: hid behind my mom with contorted shyness in constant fear of my father (or any man for that matter), my brain felt constant alarm. Danger. Be ready.

The ball can drop at any moment. I played the part of *smile and look pretty* until I couldn't. It was like trying to hold a beach ball under the water. Impossible. When it was too exhausting to hold it down another minute, my anger and aggression surfaced and I looked for control of everything—of anything—in my out-of-control world. I threw temper tantrums for hours on end until my father poured pitchers of ice cold water on my head, or my mother screamed, "What is wrong with you Joy Marie? The devil is making you do this!" or until I fell into an exhausted heap on the floor.

My soul screamed, "Help! I'm just a little girl!"

I was Jekyll and Hyde, the little girl who was very, very good and also horrid. It seemed as if the golden thread of faith was completely non-existent at times. Something that seemed even greater took its place.

Shame.

Shame crushed my dreams of being on a stage and speaking about the big God up in the sky. Our pastor's wife confirmed shame's mantra of me not being good enough no matter what as she cackled with laughter when I mustered up the courage to ask if I could sing a song at church. Shame fractured me so much that by the time I went to high school, the little girl with the big dream to speak on a stage became the teenager who strategically planned to be sick when it was my turn to give a speech in front of class.

Shame's finest form speaks to our entirety stating, "You were made wrong. You can't. You are a disappointment. You are unwanted. Unlovable. You are not good enough. You had better be sorry for everything because It is ALL your fault."

Shame loves to brand souls. The hot iron of its ownership penetrates deep and leaves a mark to let you know that you are not your own. It holds you hostage in a locked closet. Shame is a mute scream that heaps monstrous lies into brains and makes rutted paths that flow continuously deep down into our hearts as we sit in its darkness.

Shame filled me up.

I went from the "straight A" girl with twirly dresses tied with bows and on-point braided hair who led the class, to sad and depressed. I was bullied, not only at home, but at school to where I couldn't even wear my pretend smile anymore. To top it off the division between elementary and middle school broke up our little girl gang: the JLM club. It was devastating in my small world. I believed I was awful, as shame's tattoo excluded me from normal and left me backed into a corner.

One afternoon while staying inside for yet another recess to avoid the girl drama on the playground, I talked to a boy in my class who was also staying inside while no one else was around. I don't remember what I asked him but I do remember what he said. "I can't talk to you because I don't want them to stop talking to me." Now even the boys and the nerds in my class knew it. Everyone avoided me so the girls who bullied me would talk to them. Even our teacher and principal did not know what to do with me. It was as if the dark spot in me was now on me and separated me from everyone else. Months of almost daily ending up in the nurse's office, "sick" and needing to go home from school passed. I was in a dark tunnel with no way out: until a miracle happened.

The bullying was coming to an end! Our school counselor agreed to allow us feuding girls to spend time alone to talk it out in her office as requested by my friends. I was anxious and scared, but willing to try anything to gain some sort of social status out of the untouchable pit I was in. I just wanted my friends back and for this nightmare to be over! There was a glimmer of light at the end of my pre-teen tunnel.

The afternoon came. I sat alone at one end of the office and the two girls sat at the other.

"We need to turn the lights off because we can't stand to look at your face if we are going to talk to you." The lights went out in more than one way. Tears welled up and streamed down my invisible face. Hope lay down in its coffin. "unknown" and "invisible" came to the table and wrote new lies that I believed without question. The little dandelion dancing girl was an idiot with her head literally in the clouds.

Chapter 3

Little Girl Lost

I was to the point of wishing my life would end and thought about how to make it happen. The dread was too much. A tormenting darkness of unrelenting lies and shame overcame me in the middle of the night. I wrapped my bed sheets tightly around my neck in the hope of cutting off my breathing. It was my bravest physical attempt to harm myself in an unthought-out hope to stop the oppression that would not give up. Fortunately it didn't stop my breathing but it did kick start tears and courage. It wasn't pretty; I wasn't smiling, and I dishonored the family system breaking down and embarrassingly telling my mom, "I can't do this another day." Mom took me seriously, pulled me out of public school, and enrolled me in a private Christian school.

My final semester of sixth grade was a breath of fresh air mostly because of my teacher, Miss Thompson. She was young but already developing smile wrinkles. It seemed that God had permanently tattooed a smile on her face. Hers was such a different smile from the *smile and look pretty* one I wore. She didn't just smile with her mouth, her eyes followed suit. In fact, when her mouth smiled, all of her smiled along. Was she an angel or a teacher?

Her smile was one thing, but it got better. She believed in her students. She believed in me: a horrid, shy, and confused girl. Her calm and peaceful presence gave my heart hope. Wherever Miss Thompson went, encouragement followed. She shared verses from the Bible on the chalkboard and helped us memorize them, wrote personal notes of affirmation, and when students answered questions as she taught, light spilled out of her mouth. "Good job! Yes! Nice try! Keep going! Anyone else? WOW!"

The day I found a note on my desk from Miss Thompson made me feel like I had won the lottery.

You are an incredible writer.
You have a gift.
God is going to use this gift in your life.
Continue to write.
Love,
Miss Thompson

Miss Thompson's words turned the lights on in invisible me. I didn't disgust her! She noticed purpose in me. Her affirmation made me flourish in my floundering that year.

The Middle School Storm

My sixth-grade happy ending was the precursor to a middle school storm. You can imagine my disappointment when mom told me that tuition was too expensive to attend Christian school and I was going back to public school in the fall. To make matters worse, my parents' relationship continued to decline. Fighting or silence was normal. Pain and unhappiness was a regular part of life. Pop-up storms were not predictable but common inside the walls of our home, and on top of an out-of-control family, I was growing thighs and other curvy things. Could I at least control my own body? I wanted straight thighs, a flat belly, bony ankles, and a tiny butt. Boys seemed to navigate to the girls that had those assets. The opposite was happening to me. I was consumed to find an answer to slim down my chubby changing body and become like the models I saw on the cover of the magazines in the check-out line when I waited for mom to pay for groceries.

An after-school invite to a friend's house would lead me to stumble into the answer I was looking for. She explained how I could eat whatever I wanted and not gain an ounce. In fact I could lose weight.

Yes, an answer!

The magic method? Stick your finger down your throat and vomit.

Weird but OK, whatever.

I positioned myself over my friend's toilet. My pointer finger commanded the digesting after-school cookies to stand at attention and reverse course. The first few unsuccessful tries only produced tears and gagging sounds, then a dry heave, and then lo and behold the magic happened! My gag reflex ignited and accomplished the mission. The cookies were no longer a hindrance to my appearance, just a gross pool of sugar and carbs floating in front of me that I conquered.

This was an incredible discovery of control. I could have my cake and eat it too but my cake would not become me. I took the bull by the horns and learned to tether the reins of an eating disorder. Binging and purging or vomiting after a meal snowballed into stints of not eating at all, ingesting diet pills, or following my signature water and apples diet. Maybe if I could conquer the curve in my thighs I could move on to greater feats. I was finally in control and it was my little secret to keep!

Days turned into weeks and then months of skipping lunch at school, afternoons of feeling like I might pass out, and going home to binge and purge. My motivation to exercise away the curves and beat the number on the scale was high but my energy was low—literally in the toilet. Often I would give up and have dinner as if I was a skinny girl who deserved to eat. It was frustrating how the biggest change seemed to be the dark circles forming under my eyes. I thought I was a sneaky master of disguise living under the radar in order to not blow my cover of slowly starving myself to death but my sister could not be fooled. We were too close for comfort, sharing a room, a bathroom, and a sixth sense so to speak. We have the kind of relationship where we can be in a room full of people, look at each other and know without words what the other one is thinking, blurt out the same things at the same time, and finish each other's sentences. Thankfully, I could not fool her and she bravely told mom.

When confronted by mom and my grandparents, I dodged the truth and denied that I needed any kind of help. Negotiations continued and I arrogantly agreed to go to a treatment center with the stipulation that there would be a tennis court to play on when I got there. Upon arrival I quickly evaluated that I would not be playing tennis anytime soon as giant steel doors with codes and alarms welcomed me into separation from the outside world.

The Treatment Center

The treatment center staff nonchalantly officiated their routine of a new admit. I stripped naked so a female staff member could check my body inside and out for drugs or unsafe items I may be hiding. It seemed as though I had been catapulted to another dimension as I was "checked." The danger alarm sounded in my brain. A feeling of deja vu came over me: like this had happened before, and the rest of the admission seemed like a foggy dream in which I floated above the room watching myself and the staff below.

My belongings were dumped in the middle of the floor. Each item was analyzed and sorted into two piles: what I could keep and what was a tool of self harm that would be taken away. Still feeling *out of body*, I listened to the staff go over their rehearsed rules. They sounded like the teacher's voice on a Charlie Brown cartoon as they read them, *"Wa wa wa wa wa wa . . . no physical contact, no entering others' rooms, no one can enter your room . . . wa wa wa wa wa wa."* It was suffocating my control and offensive to my very, very good little girl persona. Was I in prison? What was I guilty of? What crime had I committed?

Over the course of the afternoon, I began meeting other "inmates": a tiny girl whose parents shot her up with drugs and sent her to the treatment center to "get better," a pregnant girl who endured satanic ritual abuse by her boyfriend's grandmother, and a boy who ran in a gang all over the streets of Dallas committing crimes in order to belong. My plate of *smile and look pretty* in small town Iowa to please an unhappy mom and hide an abusive dad with a side of puking to cope with curves seemed rather insignificant. As the sun set outside the "unbreakable windows," sadness set in my soul. The bubble of my small world had popped. Life on earth was painful for more than just me.

I shivered uncontrollably in an ocean of anxiety. Loneliness was my only companion the first night inside the treatment center. I was used to sharing a room and secrets with my sister until we drifted away to sleep. I was alone. Was I cold because of the temperature in my hospital room or the overwhelming unknown of life? Would sleep ever come to my racing soul? My life wasn't anything like the others I had met. Still I was desperate and at the bottom. Life was unmanageable and no longer working. How did it come to this? Was I making all of this bigger than it was? Could I just call my mom and go home? It wasn't really that bad, was it? And yet the ache in me was real. In the dark, all alone, in a locked treatment center room in the middle of Dallas, Texas—with literally everything stripped away—the ache was bigger than it had ever been. There I sat with me and my ache. I was restless and out of options. Where would life go from here? Who was I? Where was God? *Smile and look pretty* could not fix anything that night.

I started to cry, and then through my tears I quietly cried out. "God, if you are real I need to know it. I need you to show me. I need you to come and save me. Come and save me from myself." I prayed silently with my whole 15-year-old being.

I reached for a gift my grandma had given me. Maybe there was something she wrote inside that would bring me comfort. Even seeing her handwriting would bring familiarity to my unfamiliar room. My grandma was a lover of Jesus and way ahead of her time as she pioneered a business selling Jesus books, Bibles, and music out of her home in the 80s and 90s. She loved her business but she loved people a whole lot more and ended up giving most of her inventory away. Her paycheck may not have been great, but her retirement plan certainly was *out of this world!* I was a recipient of one of her giveaway bibles before I got on the plane to Dallas. I randomly opened up her gift. When

I did, my eyes fell directly on this verse, "Trust in the Lord with all your heart, lean not on your own understanding, in all of your ways submit to Him and he will make your paths straight."
-Proverbs 3:5,6 NIV.

Falling tears from an ache I could not overcome within myself turned into healing and repentance tears. I opened my heart and received the love inside of the words that I was led to. Joy flooded my soul and washed me from the inside out. Jesus came into my cold, dark hospital room with a peace that surpasses understanding. The lonely spot inside was replaced with Him. The same warmth I felt on me from God's smile during the dandelion dance as a little girl so many years ago filled the inside of me that night. Jesus saw my ache and heard my cry. He saw it all and came for me. He came into my dark with His light. The light I felt from Miss Thompson's acceptance was now a burning fire in me. I was saved from myself. Jesus came and rescued me. What felt like a standstill of forever was only moments, but those moments of deciding to trust in the Lord with all of my heart changed my life forever. I drifted off to sleep as peacefully as I had on the night when I had heard the angels sing so many years ago.

A New Beginning

I will not leave you as orphans. I will come to you.

—John 14:18 NIV

July 1, 1990, was my "gotcha day" with Jesus. He adopted me. My slate was clean. Jesus paid. He began the process of straightening out my crooked path. I couldn't wait to tell everyone.

The next morning, kids unified by a diversity of wounds filled the dining room and were served breakfast institutional style. In awe of the peace that woke me up, I floated in and sat down. Unfamiliar eyes watched my intake in the sterile environment. It was awkward but I didn't mind. Food was not my enemy anymore—proof that last night was not some concocted fantasy. There was evidence of healing. Bulimia's claws were not digging into my shoulders and weighing me down. Anorexia's slithering lies filled with empty promises that when the number on the scale was low enough and my frame was bony enough I would be happy and accepted was silenced. I lost the weight of their burdens in an instant. What a miracle!

I was not allowed to enter my room for 30 minutes after eating as a safety precaution so my food could have a chance to digest a little bit. I didn't mind; I was elated that Jesus had healed me of the eating disorder I had become addicted to. I had to tell everyone!

Since I did not have the freedom to make a phone call, I wrote letters to my mom and grandma, and composed a letter to the counselor I would be meeting soon.

Later that morning a boom box blasted in the rec room as if it was a local teen hang out. *P-Pa-Party, y'all....Heaven bound, don't you know- I'm heaven bound? Heaven bound reaching for that higher ground!* The groundbreaking rappers DC Talk pounded out Christian music's first "rad" lyrics while the girl whose parents addicted her to drugs danced, in spite of her reality. Something in my head danced right along with her and I felt a trickle of *joy*.

I wrote letters that were sent to my family and read to my counselor about the miracle Jesus had done. I was released from Jehovah Rapha (meaning, *The Lord who heals*) Treatment Center with fire in my soul. I couldn't wait to leave Dallas and go home.

Everyone in my high school would come to love Jesus and all of the problems in our family would be better because Jesus saves y'all! If *This Girl is on Fire* had been around at that time, it would have been my theme song that summer.

First on my agenda, now that I could use a phone again, was to call my dad. How amazing our relationship was going to be! Jesus had saved me and all would be well.

I dialed the push buttons, 5-1-5-8-3-2-4-3-9-2, with anxiety and excitement.

"Hello."

Words tumbled out about everything at Jehovah Rapha and ended with, "Dad, I forgive you and want to have a good relationship."

Silence.

Had we been disconnected? Was he overcome with emotion?

"Dad?"

"Dad, are you there?"

A huge space of nothing screamed loudly until finally he responded with, "That's nice for you."

His words transported me back to the sixth-grade girls chanting "We had to turn the lights off because we can't stand to look at your face." My father joined their chorus as a new place in my heart shattered.

Chapter 4

My Double Life

I returned home with new peace in Jesus and new shatters in my heart. The homecoming celebration and emotion of what had tangibly happened in Dallas that summer was short lived. Habits and systems had not changed in me or my family. My priorities of reading my Bible and telling others about Jesus were eventually derailed. It was like a summer love that grew cold when the season changed. Living for the next weekend became my main objective as I sported my big Aqua Net sprayed bangs, tucked and rolled my acid-washed jeans, and partied into my final years of high school.

My double life was reborn.

Perform. Pose. Portray strength. Be a smile-and-look-pretty Jesus-loving girl when needed and be the horrid girl with the curl in the middle of her forehead demanding, "I want what I want, and I want it now!" the rest of the time.

My parents were now in the middle of a divorce which was mostly a relief. Even though my dad was gone and all that went with him stopped, the ache inside didn't. I longed for the love of a father and searched for it in guys. My teenage brain desired instant gratification. The attention and affection of a guy, the buzz of alcohol, and belonging in the party crowd made pain and the ache inside feel better in the moment. I couldn't get enough. But parties ended and Purple Passion ran out, and when it did, I was lower than before. Still, I hit the repeat button every weekend hoping for a different result.

My sex education at home was *Don't have sex. Don't talk about sex. Don't look at sex. If sex is on TV, turn that smut off. Sex is dirty.* The horrid girl and the very, very good girl were conflicted. The status of not "doing it" with my boyfriend was not helping my social status or my ability to keep a boyfriend, but my conservative matriarchal warnings to stay away from the disgusting act did have an impact. I had no clue about sex except that it was bad and so was I, so why not?

I began dating a guy I was over the moon for. He was determined to never love. It hurt too much. He couldn't afford to put his heart out there. When he did, people died. He built walls around his heart that hid his wounds, even from himself. I saw them and was determined to break the walls down. I longed for love at any cost. High hormones motivated my longing. Our relationship went into hyperdrive. We become our own sex ed teachers. It was wild, risky, and fun until I became pregnant.

Shame came on strong to lecture me on how small, trapped, and helpless I was now. I had blown my cover by being an "easy" girl, a complete fraud, and a big disappointment to God. Shame opened the door to its familiar closet. I willingly walked in and sat down. The lights turned off once again because now even God Himself couldn't stand to look at my face. I unplugged the performance treadmill and sat frozen and alone in the dark. The dandelion dancing girl was nowhere to be found.

The First Decision

Not to decide is to decide.

—Harvey Cox

It seemed I was at a dead-end with no way out. I continued to go about life as normal, whatever that was. Thank God baggy sweatshirts were trending; my adolescent belly was no longer flush and time was running out. Not being the perfect smile-and-look-pretty girl would soon be known if I did not do something. How would I fix this?

In my conservative upbringing I had a very stern and outspoken grandfather who would say things like, "Women who abort their babies wake up in the middle of the night with nightmares of them crying."

I didn't want more nightmares but I also didn't want to be the one who shredded the family reputation—I had already bruised it pretty badly. No matter how I played out scenarios in my head, I disappointed someone. There was so much pressure. The thought of disappointing my family nauseated me more than morning sickness.

After tossing back and forth from anguish to avoidance all together I made a decision. It was settled. A date was set. An adult (other than my conservative family members) who would sign on the dotted line was found. The $250.00 it would take to keep my façade of a perfect girl was in hand. I was approved to leave school. The plan was set in motion.

The weeks leading up to the looming day of my scheduled abortion were like sitting in a theater watching my life on a screen, thinking it belonged to someone else. You know when you watch a movie you have seen, but you hope that magically there will be a different ending this time? It felt like that. I looked down at my secret bump. In two days it would be gone. This had to be a movie and not my life. Could someone please yell, *Cut?*

The Second Decision

This was no movie set, this was real life. My life. No one was acting and no one yelled cut, but a tender voice spoke.

"Are two wrongs going to make this right for you, Joy?"

If love had a voice I just heard what it sounded like inside me. It wasn't condemning or forceful. It didn't tell me, it was simply and with the utmost gentle of care posing a question with an "are you sure" attitude. I looked down at the life growing inside my belly and cried. My heart melted as the self-protective walls of performance came down with Heaven's wrecking ball of Perfect Love. What would be terminated in the coming days was my perfect girl facade, not my baby.

I gained my composure and attempted to go through a normal school day. By fifth period I was in the counselor's office spilling the beans through uncontrollable tears. My mom was notified to come so I could drop the bomb of my secret baby bump on her with the kind counselor who better deals with GPAs, class schedules, and college applications. My puffy eyes were a dead giveaway that we were not going to talk about future college plans. I looked away from my mom and at the posters of positivity filling the office walls as I broke her heart and our family system all at the same time. She cried and said, "I love you, and this does not surprise me."

Hmmm, I guess I wasn't as great at living my double life as I had thought.

I had a small list of authority figures I had to reveal my not-so-secret baby bump to. One was my grandma. The one who loved to give away Bibles. She met me with the same love my mom had.

"Joy, none of us are perfect. We love you. God made this baby. What he makes is good. We will love this little one with you."

Two down and one to go. I still had to tell my grandpa. The one I feared most.

My grandfather rarely displayed affection. He was the type of man who you knew loved you but didn't say or show it. I trembled the Saturday morning I sat with him and grandma in my room and nervously told him of the baby that would be joining our family. His words forever echo when I think back to that moment: "We love you, Joy, and we will be here for you." *Then he gave* me a hug—well, as much as stern men hug—and prayed one of the kindest prayers ever prayed for me, asking the Lord to bless me and the little life growing inside me. I experienced Jesus' grace through my grandpa that day and many days after as he stood behind the words he spoke.

The rest of my pregnancy was a messy journey of grace. In all the dysfunction of the dance between the very, very good girl who strove for perfection, keeping the peace, and pleasing people, and the horrid girl who partied and wanted what she wanted no matter what the cost, I had Jesus and he had me. That's the great grace we are given. When Jesus saves you, he writes your name in his book: not with a pencil that can be erased, but with his own blood. He did not recant his decision to adopt me as his own. Nothing could snatch me out of God's hand—certainly not pregnancy. His love flowing through my mom and my grandparents proved that.

A glimmer of light came into my skewed understanding of God's love and forgiveness as ever so slowly, my double life broke down. We explored options of keeping our baby or adoption with a gentle woman named Wanda who had a familiar presence like Miss Thompson. My childhood dream was to be a mom. I wanted this child more than anything, even though I was so young. With everything in me, for as much as I knew, I committed to loving and raising this baby in my heart while on the outside keeping the option of adoption open in order to keep my boyfriend around.

My boyfriend's guardians made it clear that he would not have a place to live if he chose to be a full-time dad. Fear aligned him with their threat. If I kept the baby he would jump ship. The physician who would deliver our baby knew much more about my pregnancy than just the due date and circumference of my belly. His wise words? "Make sure dad is in the room when the baby is born."

I took summer classes so I would not fall behind, continued to sit in the pew each Sunday as the majority of parishioners avoided me (the pregnant teen), went to my homecoming formal and football games, and held my trapper keeper in front of my protruding belly as I walked down the crowded high school hallways to class that fall, waiting to give birth.

In October of my senior year, Logan Michael was born with his dad in the room. Both of us could not have been more proud, in love with him, or scared to death to be parents as we committed to do just that.

Upon bringing Logan home from the hospital my mom made it clear that she would support me but not raise him, even though I still lived in her home. I was responsible for getting up with him in the night, as well as feeding, changing, bathing, and clothing him, and would need to ask ahead of time if I needed her to babysit. "Rude," I thought as she left to run errands.

There I sat alone with my son as he quietly slept in his bassinet. Moments of forever passed.

Seriously Mom, come back; how many errands could you possibly have?

The bigness of being a mom set in. My life would never be the same. That day I laid down my party girl agenda and picked up my son.

Like the sweet baby boy I held, 100% dependent on my care, so was I with the Lord as he continued to tenderly and ever-so-slightly straighten out my crooked life.

A Special Note

Many of you reading this right now have had an abortion or love someone who has. I see you. I have sat in tender places after sharing my story with women who did abort a child, and for the first time were able to share something they had kept hidden deep down inside them for way too long. More importantly, God sees you. I have watched the gentleness of God's tender ways lead women intimately inside of His love, and intentionally—at their pace—offer tender care as this part of their story is brought into His light. If that is you, may you know that God sees it all. God loves you. You matter to him. Your story matters to Him. Your child matters to Him. If there is *anything at all* that aches within you as you read this, Jesus is a *Wonderful Counselor and a Prince of Peace* (Isaiah 9:6). He desires to partner with you and comfort you. He will work through other trustworthy people who understand and will lovingly come alongside you as you are able to share the secret you have kept. Be brave with your heart and your story. You are precious. You are dear. You matter greatly.

Chapter 5

A Normal Life

Logan was like the sun coming out after a bad storm. How could so much love exist for someone so tiny and fragile? I thought my heart would burst open. I fell hard for this soft-skinned soul in my care, and so did others. Tremendous support from family and friends flooded us, Logan's very young and immature parents. His life showcased God's grace and love to many. Even those stuffy Baptist ladies couldn't help but dote on him. He drew attention wherever he was: the prom, basketball games, wrestling meets and my grandparents' neighborhood in Florida where my stern grandpa plopped Logan in his stroller and proudly paraded him along with his melted heart through the retirement community for all to see. God used Logan to unlock the door of my heart and connect me back to Himself. When he did, I heard the Holy Spirit's loving voice inside me a second time.

"Logan is a key for many to know Me."

Even though I could feel God's grace each time I held little Logan in my arms, the voice of the enemy kept ringing in my head, telling me the same old familiar lies.

You will never be on stage. You will never speak to women. Your dreams are selfish and will never come true. You are not good enough. No one wants to see or listen to you. They will find out that you are a fraud. Don't you see what you've done as an out-of-control teenager? You are a disappointment, even to God.

The lies made me feel small, trapped and helpless at a new level and in a new way. I listened to the lies and tried to be better on my own. Performance invited her companions of perfection, moralism, and right living along for the ride, a new form of *smile and look pretty.*

After a rocky three years of relationship ups and downs that seemed like self-sabotage cliff jumping, where sometimes we made the jump with great success and other times we slammed right into the rocky mountain bloody and bruised, we messily learned how to walk on life's path as grown-ups. Logan's dad and I married. "Normal adulthood" began to emerge. The pain of the past eventually vanished into thin air. Rhythms formed. Our sweet family continued to grow.

Full-Blown Boy Mom

Two more little boys, Collin and Trey, were born into our family. I was a full blown boy mom. These boys were and are the delight of my heart. Their lives forever changed mine and made my little-girl dream of being a mama a real life reality. Life was a whirlwind of all things boy: cars and trucks, horses, superheroes, mud and a puppy, farts and belches, tears and giggles, and oh-so-much uncontainable energy.

Mommy, mommy, mommy was a song I loved to hear, even on the most exhausting days. Snuggles paired with bedtime stories, singing, and sleepy prayers filled the routine of our nights. Laughter and squeals from innocent play filled our walls. There was fighting, competition, oh-so-many shenanigans, and many times of me losing my patience when mama had had enough; but it was home.

All three boys learned to swim early and started swimming competitively by the age of five. Long hours of daily poolside practices and out-of-town swim meets were the rhythms of our summer months. Visiting "Grandma" (aka Mom) and "Grandpa Bob" (who Mom married) were highlights as I look back. Weekends often consisted of visiting the local movie rental store to rent a movie, popping popcorn, and ordering pizza. This was our extravagance. We weren't rich with money, we were rich with each other. I was a wealthy woman. I loved God, this man, and my little boys with what I knew love to be as a busy and becoming, twenty-something woman.

We dove into adulting and doing *all the things* by working hard, purchasing a home, and growing together as a family. Our hours were fast and furious as the calendar filled and memories were filed within the blur of the days that many tell you to *enjoy because they go so fast.*

Our marriage was prioritized with date nights, writing love letters, going to marriage conferences, and having older couples as mentors. We had Christian friends. We planted a church, sang on the worship team, helped with youth ministry, hosted small groups in our home, and even eventually homeschooled. Our relationship was like Allie and Noah in *The Notebook*. We were in love with a plan to grow old together.

High-five me please! I am nailing it! Life was excellent. I had beaten my broken childhood. My boys would never experience anything close to that hideous chaos. I was making sure of it. My rebellious teenage years were a faraway land that I would never return to.

YES! Ha! Slam dunk! Do you see me now, Dad? Game over. I win! I wanted to, but never actually spoke these words to my dad; he was nowhere to be found by now.

Not-so-invisible Baggage

My husband was the hero we were all looking for. I was the pretty little mama in control. It was perfect. Well, it looked perfect. Below the surface, we were bleeding right out our emotional jugulars. I was full of anxiety and riddled with fear that spilled out in forms of control and perfection that I didn't even realize. I lived life on high alert like an emergency room nurse waiting for the next trauma to come through the door. My mind spiraled instinctively around *what-ifs and worst-case scenarios that I believed as truth and acted out in the fear they brought me.*

He was filled with grief and covered it with a big personality that showcased answers for others' problems and no problems of his own.

It has been said that 85% of marriage issues stem from negative childhood experiences. If that's the case, we carried bags stuffed full of that 85% right into our first day and packed it away never to be remembered again. It was a good try—a great try actually—but stuffing pain and avoidance of it only goes so far. It leaked out ever so slowly into the present through his living large and covering up, and my control and perfection. We did our best. The years rolled along with all the elements of a perfect storm rolling right along with us.

A NORMAL LIFE

Have you ever been outside right before a fierce storm? It's incredibly calm. Eerily calm. The sky is a most peculiar green. Parts of the sky are full of sunshine and others are black as night. Clouds move quickly. Birds stop chirping. The wind stands still. In an instant the temperature drops from muggy heat to almost a chill. You know something is about to blow. I could feel it in my bones and rallied my girlfriends, "Please pray, something is stealing the peace out of our home."

I was no stranger to storms. There was a storm brewing. My gut felt it when I was sitting with my husband at the local coffee shop. Friends said hello as if they were in a vacuum. A heaviness rested on us. What was it? "My attentive superhero is right here and a million miles away." I thought. It was getting lonelier every day. Storm warnings rolled across my ticker as an internal radar forecasted the coming dread.

That night I sat on my bathroom floor and read *Facing Your Giants* by Max Lucado cover to cover through the night, looking for ways to ward off a giant storm.

You know your giant. He taunts you with bills you can't pay, people you can't please, habits you can't break, failures you can't forget, and a future you can't face. But just like David, you can face your giant, even if you aren't the strongest, the smartest, the best equipped, or the holiest. You could read David's story and wonder what God saw in him, He fell as often as he stood. But for those who know the sound of a Goliath, David gives this reminder: Focus on giants - you stumble. Focus on God - your giants tumble. —Max Lucado, *Facing Your Giants*[1]

---

[1] Max Lucado. "Facing Your Giants - God Still Does the Impossible," UpWords, The Teaching Ministry of Max Lucado, 2024, https://maxlucado.com/products/facing-your-giants-god-still-does-the-impossible/.

"Lord, what is my giant? Whatever it is, I am ready to face it." I prayed.

Unrest

In January I want to hibernate under blankets with a steady supply of comfort food and not move until spring. Snowbirds who fly south are the smart ones.

Hibernation was clearly not an option with the needs of a fast-growing family. My minivan braved the elements like a champ as I ran the errands that don't take a long winter's nap. I cranked the heater high and the radio loud. A familiar pastor's voice attracted my attention as it resounded through the speakers, "I want to know Christ and the power of his resurrection." I drove home slowly. The dread of the bitter cold that would meet me when I opened my van door and the message still playing on the radio compelled me to linger in the driveway. Every word coming out of the speakers captivated my heart as if the voice were speaking only to me. "Know Christ. Know the power of resurrection."

Compelled to find the verse in Philippians in print before the moment was gone, I exited the warmth and ran inside. Black ink underlined the crisp page that would become so tattered and torn.

> *I want to know Christ and the power of his resurrection, to share in the fellowship of his suffering, becoming like him in his death, and so, somehow, to attain resurrection from the dead.*
>
> —Philippians 3:10,11 NIV (paraphrased)

I did know Christ. My soul cried for more. Going to church, praying at meals, checking off my almost-daily time with the Lord in His word, and doing *all the things* was not enough. I was going through the motions. It felt shallow. I longed for depth. Something remarkable and extraordinary, just like in bible times. I was bored with American Christianity. I wanted to know Christ and the power of resurrection.

It was as if my soul shouted, *If you are a shepherd, come and corral my drifting heart. If you are a Wonderful Counselor, I could use some divine therapy. If you are a friend, Jesus, let's hang out: do coffee, get our schedules together and make it happen. I want to know you as Father.* Lord knows that area of me could use some work—#daddyissues. *And Healer, come and heal, there is so much hurt and pain. Oh, and Jesus, while you're at it, I want to see resurrection in my day. I want to see dead things come to life. You said in your Word that those who believe will do the things that you did when you were here on the earth and even greater things. So how about some of that resurrection power, Jesus!* My soul cried with a bit of sass, *Hey Jesus, throw down some resurrection power and how about a cape to go with it!*

Philippians 3:10 warmed the cold night while the brewing of a coming storm continued.

Chapter 6

March 5, 2007

March 5, 2007

I never checked my husband's phone. I had no reason to. This morning we scurried around getting ready to take our boys swimming at the local gym, and I happened to walk by his phone resting on our dresser as the screen lit up. I glanced at it. The words froze me. My giant prayer about what my giant was lit up like a billboard. The storm commenced as I saw a revealing text from another woman on my husband's phone.

Remembering and writing this is like asking me to go and relive the worst nightmare I have ever had. I have gotten up five times, stared at my computer screen, and for months have thought of every other obligation I could think of rather than giving words to this day, March 5, 2007: the day I learned what it feels like to be a refugee in my own life. In a moment, everything that was safe and known a minute earlier was now terrifying, even down to our home itself.

Adultery was the tip of the iceberg that our perfect little Christian family cruise-ship voyage crashed into that day. On the surface, two hurting kids were attempting to be one as adults by doing all the right things. It was like we were furnishing and decorating a home so beautifully and giving no attention to the fact that the foundation was cracked and the walls were about to cave in. The storm screamed that buried pain is not sustainable over a lifetime and a healthy adult life cannot be built on the foundational cracks of hidden hurt from childhood forever.

Under the surface were layers and layers of suppressed trauma frozen in each of us, begging to be surfaced and healed. That's the thing with icebergs; they appear small on the surface but underneath looms 90 percent of their mass.

I confronted my husband. He put it off as some sick joke from a friend at work. I knew better. This was answered prayer.

Adrenaline rushed, fight, flight, or freeze through me as I lay on the floor. Is this a multiple choice test? I choose D, all of the above. I wept uncontrollably as he stood staring blankly over the pitiful pile of not-enough-me on our living room floor grasping at the fibers, as if holding on to them would sustain me in that moment. Small, trapped, and helpless screamed at me while I laid frozen there, until my strong will kicked in and led me to fight. Without thought I bolted out the front door and ran across the street where an elder from our church worked. Maybe he could help.

"You need to go home and figure this out with your husband," was his "help."

Enraged and embarrassed, I ran back into the storm. Instincts to protect my babies went into full gear. But what was I protecting them from?

I needed to get them safe—and NOW! I called for help.

"No!?!" was the first word out of Mom's mouth. She could not believe me initially: not our family's superhero. That is not how the story is supposed to go. My emotional state convinced her. Within a couple of hours she and my stepfather were sitting on our couch. I curled up in a ball like a little girl in Mom's lap, sobbing uncontrollably: sobs from the present and from so very long ago.

Running From Pain

We packed up and went to Mom and Bob's house thinking this would bring peace. Pain followed me all the way to their house and didn't let up for a second. In a couple of days we packed back up and went home with pain hot on our trail.

Get my babies out of pain! Save my babies! was all I could think of. But no matter where I went or what I did, the giant of pain was there breathing down our necks, screaming in our sleep, haunting the sunniest day. I called every counselor and pastor I could find to get this figured out. I ran to counselors and pastors, asking—no, *BEGGING*—for the secret remedy to get life quickly back to normal, excellent, and perfect. There were none.

In fight, flight, or freeze mode, the brain and body will return to a normal state when the threat or perceived threat has subsided. The rawness of this new reality kicked in intense survival responses round the clock in those first weeks. Anger raged in me as a broken-down marriage made threats on any kind of future for our family. In survival mode, I attempted every possible action that I knew to dig my babies out of the debris the storm surge caused. I wanted to protect my boys from the fact that they lived in a busted-up world. I wanted them to remain innocent, looking in bible story books at Daniel in the den of lions drawn in cartoon form with a smile on his face, petting the friendly lions smiling by his side. The cover was blown. The den of lions was dark, filled with bones, the stench of feces, and frightening echoes of devouring roars. I wanted them to know that authority could be trusted. Family and home are safe and secure. I wanted them to avoid any kind of pain that resembled my childhood, and there I was, smack dab in the failure of that goal.

My husband and I separated. I kept running in every way possible. Literally. I dropped 20 pounds in weeks. I was on a mission to find that priceless remedy to fix the pain we were in.

I remember walking into one of my many counselors' offices. He was wild and reckless. *And how does that make you feel* was not part of his therapeutic regimen. I let him know that I had made a promise to myself that my children would *NEVER* be children of divorce. He looked me straight in the eye and without hesitation said, "So you have pride issues." Ugh. His words were piercing, but I liked him. There was no B.S.

Hard truth was confronting me: we are all hard wired for struggle upon arrival; my own birth proved that. It was impossible to keep my boys from it. As a mom, I would have given my life to keep them from pain. The truth smacked me in the face; from a skinned knee to a fragmented home, they will experience brokenness, have problems, and ache. They are sinners, prone to question, wander, and rebel from God. Jesus was a necessity; he came for real pain: our pain. The cross was bloody for reasons I was just beginning to understand and would rather avoid.

In a minute, my life went from being the church-planting, small-group leader—who poured into others—to a devastated woman not knowing how to muster up the strength to get up off the bathroom floor, stop crying, and put precooked chicken strips on a baking sheet for dinner. *I* made meals for those in need and prayed for those with life's blows. The tables turned.

My sister lightened the heaviness on the evening of our wedding anniversary. What was supposed to be a night out surprising my husband and seeing one of our favorite bands was now a night I wasn't sure I could make it through. She brought her specialty: endless energy and laughs. Anyone else with that level of happiness in the midst of my sadness would have pissed me off. She pulled it off. We both laughed that night and my boys did too. She was like coming up to the surface and breathing fresh air after holding your breath underwater. It helped for a while until the sadness swept over me once again. I went into my bedroom and cried myself to sleep in an exhausted heap with the lights on as my sweet sister laid next to me singing the same sobbing melody I was while holding me tight. I slept deep in the warmth of her love in our home. I didn't know where I was or how long it had been when I woke up to joyful boys and a clean house. What a gift she is.

"Get ready, I'm coming to pick you and your boys up and take you out for dinner." This was my friend's greeting when I answered the phone. I let go of pride, humbled down, and agreed to receive: something I would awkwardly learn to do more of as the days and weeks unfolded.

I eventually realized there was no quick fix. No person. No answer. No counselor. No book. No magic prayer. There was not a long enough run that would move pain and sadness far away. There was nothing that would instantaneously put life back together. The one thing that was there was pain. Constant. Steady. Real.

The Megaphone of Pain

Pain is God's megaphone to a deaf world.
—C.S. Lewis[2]

Pain was picking up its megaphone and screaming loud to gain my full attention.

I went from being at home and homeschooling my boys to enrolling them back in school and picking up a full-time schedule of cleaning homes and offices. When I wasn't cleaning or caring for them I was in counseling, clearing my mind with a long run, or leaning hard on the support of friends and family. Regardless of the day's schedule, pain continued to use its megaphone to scream through my days.

In pain, I made one really good decision: not to make any major decisions for six months. This allowed me to put aside the constant pressure to find an answer to fix the issue(s) when there seemed to be zero solutions. Sometimes it felt like a waiting game for me to *buck up, get better,* and *get over it.* It hurt so bad. That wasn't possible or even reasonable. This six-month perspective took the pressure off and gave pain a voice. The solution at hand was to listen to what pain had to say and explore its viewpoint. There was no plan to stay together or get divorced. This gave us both space to live in pain and let it teach us. It was forever of a short time.

In those months, God started exposing my crooked thinking. The messages of childhood lies that were recorded inside my mind seemed to be set on a sad repeat playlist. They sang the well-known chorus over and over: *If I could just be . . . skinnier,*

---
[2] C.S. Lewis, *The Problem of Pain*, HarperCollins 2001, pp. 88-89.

sexier, funnier, prettier, richer, friendlier, a better wife, friend, lover, mother, daughter, sister, friend, a better Christian, have a nicer house, a cleaner house, a more inviting house. If I could just be more involved, energetic, more adventurous, if I was smarter. If I could just be like so and so and have what so and so has, if my husband could be like so and so . . ." on and on the list would go and end with, then I would be_____. Fill in the big fat blank: **GOOD ENOUGH.**

The lies planted in me as a little girl while running at an exhausting pace on a performance-based treadmill to make mom happy and keep dad away were now the mantra of thirty-something me. No matter how hard I tried through the years, I could never be good enough. These beliefs were concreted in like cement. I lived them out daily without even knowing it. They lived right underneath the surface of the iceberg we had crashed into. Here in the season of pain using its megaphone, they broke off and floated up where they were exposed.

Feeling pain and uprooting lies were hard. I was awake and aware as the deception I instinctively lived out from the past became known in my present. What about my Philippians 3:10 prayer of knowing Christ and resurrection? My emotional heartache was so bad at points that it felt physical: like my heart was physically breaking. Panic attacks could come on at any given moment, whether the middle of the night or day and felt like hands around my neck squeezing and sucking the life right out of me. This was suffering and more like death than resurrection.

I continued unpacking bag after emotional bag filled with the 85% I had buried deep through professional counseling, lay counseling, meeting with my pastor, talking with friends and family, and lying on my floor with my Bible and journal discovering all the things my soul had kept under lock and chain.

When I couldn't unpack another thing I put on my tennis shoes and hit the ground running to keep my sanity.

Pain Gained a Companion

Pain was my master teacher that would not relent from its long lectures. Pain stabbed at the grocery store, at my boys' school events, on birthdays and holidays. Living in a small town made me feel like the paparazzi followed me everywhere I went, now solo. It was exhausting to show up in life. When people avoided me it felt lonely. When people asked how I was doing and engaged I felt exposed. Pain sometimes took my breath away.

Pain was the main event that would not sing a finale whether my boys were with me or with their dad. The concert of pain continued its show even though the songs changed and were like a headbanger's ball when they were with their dad. There was nothing else, nor could there ever be anything else. Pain was the whole thing: the entirety of life. It was the mountain in front of me that blocked my view to see anything else—until one afternoon after a long run.

I sat on my back deck and realized something else in the steady drip of pain: the watermelon I was eating as my post-run snack was amazingly sweet! I paused, noticed the color, taste, texture, and how it connected with my taste buds. How amazing was it that my taste buds differentiated it between thousands of other flavors! My soul praised the Lord. Taste and see. A trickle of joy. Small healing. Self-aware. Present. God-aware. New beginnings. A little light breaking in while doing the hard work of feeling pain: the hard and right choice. I sat in stillness on the back deck noticing the many layers of chipped paint on the wood and awaked to my own inhale and exhale, how warm the sun felt on my bare shoulders, and how painful grieving losses and truth telling was. Opposing feelings—joy and pain—sat down in my heart and coexisted together. My willing spirit and weak flesh welcomed them in. I felt life. I was alive. It was good. Tasting watermelon provided an education that no classroom could. Could there be dandelion dancing again?

Chapter 7

Write the Pain

It is important to gain self-knowledge as part of spiritual growth, to know and believe in yourself means you can know and believe in God. Fill yourself first and then only will you be able to give to others. Knowledge of yourself produces humility and knowledge of God produces love.

—St. Augustine

As one grows in prayer one also grows in the knowledge of oneself, and if not in one's sinfulness, then certainly in the potential sinfulness. It brings about a real understanding of what St. Philip Neir said: "There go I but the grace of God." And as time goes on, it's much easier to accept the weaknesses of others because deep down there is at least the potential for sinfulness in oneself. We are all human; we all have the same human weaknesses."

—Mother Teresa, *The Simple Path*

While Mom lay sleeping on her hospital bed my heart felt the same joy and pain collision I had felt on my back deck so many years ago: memories with her that were just as sweet as that watermelon tasted, and pain with her that hurt as much as the breakdown in my marriage. I wondered if she was sorting through these things too while she slept?

Joy and Pain Living

Joy and pain made themselves at home in my heart. They gave my wounded soul rest, my shattered heart a place to grieve, and my flatlined dreams air. Piece by piece, lie by lie, wound by wound, Jesus met me and offered me a drink of Himself: Living Water.

Months went by. My husband and I were still separated but attempted communication that was a wild roller coaster ride. Up, up, up we would go ever so slowly with a hint of hope and a spark of joy. We would get to the top of a hill with a moment of peace and then slam! Down we would go as the hurt plummeted us once again. Betrayal felt like a knife that bulls-eyed my heart and twisted every little chance it got. Trust was shattered to pieces. There were so many fragments and shards of glass everywhere in our lives. I wrestled with the question, what was the difference between being caught and sorry and true repentance? I looked for the answer with every move he made. I was an undercover agent looking for evidence, following clues, and gathering facts to answer the question in my heart. I longed to solve the case and know: repentant or sorry. Could my jaded lens even see if he was being truthful and repentant? Out of my hurt could I be objective? Betrayal is a bricklayer that builds walls around your heart. Rejection is the forest field that blocks the soul from ever wanting to step into the vulnerable place of intimacy and trust ever again.

The ride circled upside down and all around over and over. What would it look like to get off at the end of all of this? I really wanted off the ride.

With an unknown future and ups and downs in the present, I kept a rhythm of taking care of my boys, continuing my cleaning business, going to counseling, talking with friends and family, running off my frustrations, seeking counsel from my pastor, and writing.

Almost daily, I went into my bedroom, closed the door, and laid down on the outdated shaggy brown carpet with my bible, pen, and notebook. The Holy Spirit imparted love into my soul. With an open heart and a scribing pen, I willingly received. I wrote and wrote and wrote. The Lord met me on the floor of my bedroom and taught me how to encounter Him. These times were fuel in my tank. They kept me going. I couldn't get enough.

May 28, 2007 (Journal Entry: Condensed)

I walk into the depths of me to see reality for what it is. I can no longer forfeit what lives beyond my walls of self-protection. I'm out of options. Life is no longer working. I hit a fork in the road and left the path of normal. It was liberating. I felt more like myself than I ever had and then the lights went out.

The dark terrified me and showed me that normal was a facade hiding the spiritual battlefield we are born on amidst the sterile hospital, with smiling parents, flowers, smiles, balloons, and gifts.

The dark exposed good on my own is wretched; godly without God is a fabricated, legalistic, religious, cover up in which

AND SO SOMEHOW

I create my own cute little Jesus who may be used at my disposal. Accomplishments are dust collectors on my *Look at me* trophy shelf, or they are stuffed in my closet of shame—either way: pride.

Lustful mind games lurk in dark places of my mind-the hometown of temptation. Here, the local bartender mixes up a cocktail pulled from choice distilled lines of: One last time, just one more, tomorrow, on Monday, after this happens, before I have a chance to belly up to the bar. Day after day after day.

I'm exhausted, beaten down, and filled with grief. I'm filthy from wallowing in the pig pen of me. I ache from lack of sustenance. I'm at the end of myself. Where can I go? It's so dark.

I'm face down, focused only on myself. But I sense a glimpse of something. I look up. There is light. I inch closer. It is The Light. Old thinking patterns plead with me to abandon mission and return to the comfort of what I know. Time stands still. I am in the Light of God's Glory. All is known. Every breath thunders out of my chest. In the climax of the moment, I sense someone else is there. I am not alone. Who is it? I muster the courage to find out. It's Jesus. I gaze into His eyes. All that is within me comes to a hush. My heart calms from pounding to a purr. My breath synchronizes with . . . The Breath of Life. The Light changes from terrifying to intoxicating. He asks me: "Will you come?"

Will you come and leave the trouble you have found and that has found you? Will you walk away from what eats your soul? Will you depart ways with the demanding author-self that writes the same defeating lines over and over? Will you come and break ties with addictions, strongholds, and generational baggage you have been carrying? Will you relinquish ties with deception? Will you come?

His invitation gets personal. He speaks my name, and words I have longed to hear my whole life. He calls me child, baby girl and his darling. I am captivated. I cannot turn away. My heart is melting. "Yes, I will come!"

God's Response and Loving Reminder

My *"YES!"* to His question, *Will you come?* was a cliff jump into the ocean of God's love. It reminds me of an opportunity I had to snorkel while vacationing on the island of St. John in recent years. You see, I love water; I just don't like getting wet. When I was about five years old I was undertaken by an ocean wave. Spoiler alert: I didn't drown, but it was very traumatic. It's rare for me to completely immerse myself in water.

Peer pressure and a once-in-a-lifetime opportunity dragged me onto the chartered boat that morning. I pleaded with the Lord to not let me die on the boat ride out to sea. My heart beat wildly: *How would my obituary read? Eaten by sharks? Still diving for remains? Frozen to death by fear?*

The only visible piece of land at this point was a coral reef sticking out of the water like a little mountain peak—and it was illegal to touch it. Captain Ollie slowed the boat as we approached it. The morning conversations had educated us about our wild-hearted captain. Ollie was from the mainland but had moved to the island in search of adventure. Tanned leather skin and sun-bleached hair that would be dark in a colder climate gave him the stereotypical look of a "fun in the sun" thrill seeker. A "no worries" attitude verified his features as he confidently brought the boat to a stop, gave instructions, and handed out gear. My fellow explorers excitedly put it on and dove in while I self-talked my way out of a full blown panic attack. I would soon be the last one in the boat. Hesitantly, I put on my gear and decided to acquire a dose of *no worries* from Mr. Thrill Seeker himself.

"Do you ever get scared out here?" I asked.

I already knew his answer, which would likely be followed by a look of pity. Without hesitation he looked intentionally out at the ocean, paused hard, looked me in the eyes, and put his face mask on. "Every day." he replied and jumped in, preaching a sermon, in a second.

With a loud shriek I jumped too. I felt tiny in the limitless ocean as I plopped in. My face mask filled with water. Having a panic attack while breathing through a snorkel was especially difficult. I made adjustments and had a reassuring pep talk with myself. My breathing settled. Courage gave me a permission slip to put my face in the water and look down. My heart exploded. God's creation in the deep is breathtaking. The water was crystal clear. Shoals of fish swam and sea turtles calmly circled about. I was in the real-time movie set of *Finding Nemo*. The coral reef was a gorgeous treasure under the water. Plants swayed to and fro with the rhythm of the waves. The sunlight reflected on the grains of sand making it look like Heaven-swept residue from the streets of gold to the bottom of the sea. I could not help but worship the Magnificent Creator as brilliant colors in intricate patterns on hundreds of living creatures floated below. My "Yes" to Jesus' question, "Will you come?" was like the dive off of Ollie's boat into the ocean. Oh what I would have missed if I had said *no* and stayed in my boat of comfort.

Chapter 8

Me? A Princess.

*Listen, daughter, pay attention,
and forget about your past.
Put behind you every attachment to the familiar,
even those who once were close to you!
For your royal Bridegroom is ravished
by your beautiful brightness.
Bow in reverence before him, for he is your Lord!*

—Psalm 45:10,11 TPT

I jumped in the ocean of God's love each time my journal opened. Love, connection, and belonging to Him grew in me. The Holy Spirit guided my pen page after page. I cried my tears and poured out my heart. He spoke through words in my spirit. I captured them on the page. Was I experiencing what the woman who burst into the Pharisee dinner party experienced with Jesus?

Jesus was at a Pharisee's (high level religious leader) party, when a *certain immoral woman* came uninvited with a jar of expensive perfume (Luke 7). She knelt at Jesus' feet, weeping and wiping her tears off with her hair. She kissed his feet over and over, and poured the perfume on them. The Pharisee was repulsed. Didn't Jesus know how sinful this woman was?! I'm guessing the tension in the room could have been cut with a knife. And I'm also guessing the woman had no clue about it; she was motivated and captivated. It says that Jesus reads Simon's (the Pharisee's) thoughts. He responded to them with a parable of how two men had debts they could not pay off. One a small debt the other a large one. The man who loaned the money forgave both debts. Jesus asked Simon: "Who do you suppose loved him more after that?" He answered, "The one with the larger debt." Jesus gave Simon a thumbs up while turning to the woman and saying, "Do you see this woman?"

Could the party get more radical? Jesus broke all sorts of cultural norms of that time with one question. He got personal with a woman. Perhaps for the first time in her life she is seen. Jesus goes on to affirm her actions of feet washing, kissing, and anointing. He calls her out in love and proclaims to the dinner guests "Her many sins are forgiven." Then he intimately proclaims to her, "Your sins are forgiven." The dinner guests are thinking, "Who is this that forgives sins?" They are a mixture of perplexed and indignant. All the chains must have fallen completely off the woman as Jesus declared to her, "Your faith has saved you, go in peace."

This is one of my favorite accounts in the bible. It showcases intimacy with Jesus in so many ways. He *reads the thoughts* of the Pharisee and after he does the account goes from calling him *a Pharisee* to calling him by his name: *Simon*. He personally walks Simon through the confusion of what is happening that is outside of everything he has ever been taught. Jesus patiently tells a non-threatening external story to help him understand. Then he cuts to the chase and raises a love banner for all to see over the woman. Intimately, he looks at her. He asks everyone to see her. Can you imagine that look? He doesn't gloss over the fact that there has been a ton of sin in her life. He acknowledges it and that is why healing waters of forgiveness need to flow. She is forgiven. He uses her actions as an example every heartbeat in the room can follow. To seal the moment the secret ingredient of faith is brought up. She had faith. Faith to believe in him. Faith to risk everything that night and come. Faith to not hesitate a second longer but to act on her faith. When her loving actions, past sin, and Jesus collided in one room, her chains fell off. She was free. Peace was the parting gift as she left the party that night. Oh what she would have missed had she stayed home in her solo party of fear and isolation.

In faith I brought my tears and jar of oil to Jesus. Jesus swept up the pile of teary me from the floor and stood me upright. I learned to live in the middle of a broken heart and a healing life. My energy returned. I wondered if the party-crashing woman and I had that in common too. Faith, forgiveness, and peace as the past still affected the present. Did she too experience joy while not everything in life was fixed? Did she entertain true confidence bit by bit? Did she have little light-bulb moments throughout her day that maybe what God has to say about her is the truth? I think we could have been great friends. I feel a coffee date needing to be scheduled between us on our eternal calendars.

In the mix of heartbreak and healing, God captured my princess heart as only a loving Father could. I felt like Cinderella. Her stepsisters ripped her ballgown to shreds and magically she was still given a chance to go to the ball and meet her prince charming. But then the clock struck midnight. She ran for home one-shoed in a ballgown that turned to shreds once again. She had met her prince, gazed into his eyes and danced. Was it all a dream? Would she ever be in his arms again? The wait seemed like forever. Until there was a knock on the door.

October 4, 2007 (Journal Entry Condensed Version)

Father, you are Prince Charming, knocking on the door of my heart. Come in. Speak to me.

Everything is going to be alright. I rejoice over you with singing. I quiet you with my love. I stand for you. I'll never leave you or forsake you. I was pierced for your darkest hour, deadliest secret, most controlling addiction. I was crushed for your sin. The punishment I took brings you peace. (Breathe it in.) I saw everything you would do and what would be done to you when I hung on the cross. My scars bring us together and heal you.

I am your Father. What do you need? Tell me. I own the cattle on a thousand hills. I will open the flood gates of Heaven and pour out so much blessing, you will not have enough room for it. I am your rich and powerful Father. I own everything. It is all mine. I make you great and give you strength.

I am your deliverer. You are being delivered. You have suffered. I am making you strong, firm, and steadfast. Take off your filthy rags and put on the wardrobe I give, fit for a princess in my Kingdom. Seek me and my Kingdom. My Kingdom is in you now—on the earth as it is in Heaven. In Heaven where there are mansions. I went away to build one for you. I will come back. You will one day be home. We are and will be together forever.

Someday is here. My Prince has come and rescued me. When I see myself in his reflection, I do not disgust myself. No man can fill His place. His words of truth are my missing glass slipper that slides perfectly on. *My Cinderella story is you*, God. I listen and scribe the restorative truth he speaks.

You are still my dancing girl with flowers. I am as present in the moment you twirled on your front lawn with a dandelion bouquet, as I am now. I saw then all that you would endure and every choice you would make that would turn you away from my love. You are still mine. I have summoned you. I have called you by name. I have ransomed you. You are precious. I love you.

Wounds matter. I know how much they matter. I suffered and endured the cross. It did not feel good. Just like my time on the cross, your pain will not be forever. You are safe in a protective cocoon of healing. Your former self is shedding off and making way for new life. You are growing wings. When you think you cannot stay any longer, you will be ready. You will fly. Linger in healing. It is good. It is my best for you and exactly what you need. There is a specific purpose, a higher calling that I have for you. Hold on.

Jesus wooed me on the dance floor of abundant life with Him and captivated me with truth where I danced free and without care. His embrace healed and restored me. I didn't feel quite as small, trapped, and helpless anymore. This wild romance of the Father's love consumed me. I was knowing Christ, just like Philippians 3:10 stated. I wanted to stay in Jesus' love, hearing him speak sweet affirmations to me forever. I had come to discern his voice by now and loved the sound of it in my soul.

Take up your cross.

It was unmistakable. It was his voice minus the sweet affirmations. These words seemed to bring the divine romance to a screeching halt. They felt like my alarm clock on a rainy Monday morning when I'm snuggled deep in my comfy covers. *Please, just five more minutes! Can we hit the snooze on that?* I thought to myself. He spoke again.

AND SO SOMEHOW

Take up your cross. I held you while the fire burned. I won't ever let go. Do you see these ashes? I will do something beautiful with them. It's time to move on.

Chapter 9

Two Steps Forward, One Step Back

*Return, (O Israel), to the Lord your God,
for your sins have brought you down.
Bring your confessions, and return to the Lord.
Say to him, "Forgive all our sins and graciously receive us,
so that we may offer you our praises.
Assyria cannot save us, nor can our warhorses.
Never again will we say to the idols
we have made, 'You are our gods.'
No, in you alone do the orphans find mercy."
The Lord says, "Then I will heal you of your faithlessness;
my love will know no bounds, for my
anger will be gone forever."*

—Hosea 14:1-4 NLT

I wish I could say taking up my cross went well. The taste of freedom was intoxicating. It was like I was turning around and screaming, *Noooooooo!* into my past and telling shame and lies who's boss. When Jesus gave grace and mercy, I drank it in. When He asked for surrender and obedience, I hesitated.

As I wrestled with taking up my cross and what that even meant, the six-month *making no major decisions* deadline came. I was still conflicted. Was I seeing *sorry or repentance?* I did not know as I sifted through actions of the past and present. God was building me up but I was still so incredibly fragile and weak.

Ever so discreetly an older man took notice of my now-fit and firm body, growing confidence, and my incredible state of vulnerability. The gray drip of conversation with him turned into more. He noticed me. He saw me. He affirmed me. It was a complete counterfeit that looked and felt like all the words I heard Jesus tell me that hid inside my journal. I was tired of pain and bored of healing. I was feeling and it was real. *Real* felt vulnerable and butted heads with *smile and look pretty*. I loved my time with Jesus on the floor with my journal but it felt like the rest of the world was living their best lives while I was stranded in pain. My head knew this was wrong and my selfish heart vetoed its logical campaign to flee the situation. Instead of taking up my cross, I lay down in bed with this man.

Conviction was strong. God's love didn't move—I separated from it. It was awful. The momentary intoxication this pain numb of an affair brought could not hold a candle to what I had experienced with the Lord. After a period of months, I broke off the relationship. There I was again with a steady diet of pain. Maybe this is where I belonged. Maybe I would remain stuck here. Maybe I deserved it. If I had been good enough in the first place my husband wouldn't have been unfaithful, right? If I hadn't been a disappointment to God himself after all the love and care he had given me, I wouldn't be feeling this awful. If only I wasn't here regretting my choices and half healed. Small, trapped, and helpless returned. Would I ever learn?

The Example I Needed

Many years ago a woman excitedly boarded a train. A young woman filled the seat next to her. The two exchanged friendly pleasantries to pass the time. Both were going to meet the men in their lives: one, her military husband, the other, her military lover. The more they chatted, the more they had in common right down to the first name of the men they loved. Time passed as miles were crossed. I'm not sure if it was curiosity or simple pleasantry but the woman with a boyfriend pulled out a shocking truth neither were looking for through a picture in her purse. The boyfriend and husband were the same man. As the train covered miles, devastation became their final destination.

The devastated wife was my grandmother. A train ride changed her whole life.

Grandma survived that heart-wrenching blow. She eventually married a man named Lyle, my grandfather. They lived a life of trials, triumphs, tests, and testimony together.

Grandma became a follower of Jesus while raising her young family, when a kind man tapped on her front door one day to share the love of Jesus with her. Grandma loved Jesus, was a Holy Spirit-filled woman of faith, my beautiful heroine, and my dear friend. If you ask me who the most beautiful woman I have ever met is, I will tell you without hesitation, hands down: my grandma, Betty Jean Miller.

Grandma loved the Lord with all her heart. She led many to Jesus, prayed, and taught the word of God by the way she lived her life. Even still, Grandma lived apologizing for much of what she did and for who she was.

Much Will Be Required

On a car ride together, Grandma shared with me that the Holy Spirit spoke to her and said, *Much will be required of you, child.* On Christmas Eve, 1999, we crowded in our family physician's exam room and found out why. Grandma had been losing weight, unable to keep food down, and living in a state of fatigue and pain. The familiar face of our doctor entered the room. Over the years he had written prescriptions for our common ailments and performed our yearly check-ups. This was the same doctor that said, "Make sure Dad is in the room." when I was about to become a teen mom. The grim look on his face was unfamiliar. He delivered Grandma's diagnosis of pancreatic cancer with a prognosis of two months to live with tears in his eyes. She smiled through tears knowing her day of saying hello to her Savior and goodbye to her family was soon approaching.

I hesitated when calling Grandma after that. It was a usual call, one that I loved to make, but the normal greeting of *Hi Grandma, how are you?* didn't work. I knew how she was. She was dying. Her body hurt. What would I say when I heard her voice? Why did I feel nervous to talk to my grandma?

The Lord led me to Luke 8:50 in the bible. *Don't be afraid; just believe, and she will be healed.* I drank His Word up like hope. It gave me the courage to dial her number.

"Hi Grandma, it's so good to hear your voice."

"You too, Honey."

"How are you feeling, Grandma?"

"I'm ok. I'm ready to go home and be with Jesus." Her voice cracked as she attempted to finish. "I'm just so sad that I won't get to see your sweet boys grow up."

The line was silent on both ends. The realization that the healing my grandma was receiving was a heavenly one set in. I couldn't imagine a world without her and I didn't want to.

Grandma's Final Days

"Becky, wake up! We need to find the scripture that says Jesus holds the keys to death!"

My sleepy aunt fulfilling her shift by grandma's bedside sat up in a startled fog, "What's wrong mom, do you need more Morphine? Do you want me to call the nurse to come?"

Grandma was looking for something beyond the pain numb a narcotic could provide her dying body. Her fingers thumbed through the worn out pages of her bible in the wee hours of the night. She was adamant to find the scripture pressing within her that Jesus held the keys to death.

Tears of frustration spotted the pages as she scanned the word of God hoping for an illumination on the truth pounding within her. After another refusal for Morphine my exhausted aunt took the bible and began looking for the scripture herself.

"Becky, did you know, they beat Jesus until he was unrecognizable?"

By now grandma was sobbing. "You couldn't even tell he was a human." She managed to speak through her tears.

The present reality of suffering Grandma was enduring and Jesus collided. Grandma's tears were not for herself. She was crying for Jesus. His suffering was touching hers. It resurrected a strength within her. She was encouraged. Jesus had gone before her to make a way. "I can do this!" she proclaimed with resolution in her voice.

She spoke with fearless unshakeable faith in her final days until her words were no more.

Dying brings the opposite of life. Bearing life into the world is a labor of contractions that grow stronger and closer together until one cry is heard. Eternal birthing rooms are filled with breaths that become weaker and farther apart until there is nothing left and many cries are heard.

Mom lovingly prepared a room in her home as grandma's eternal birthing room to live out her final days in. Here the tables turned. We did what she had taught us to do her whole life long: love without limit. We tended to Grandma's dying body, swabbing her mouth with sponges that resembled suckers, massaging her dehydrated limbs with lotion, and replenishing cool cloths on her forehead when her fever spiked while her soul did the hard work of departure. She was usually somewhere else sorting things out with Jesus, I imagine, but every so often she woke up. When she did, we squeezed in precious last moments to share our hearts, read scripture verses, pray, and sing as her hands raised in worship.

Her last day was precious: just as precious as the birth of my children. Our family gathered as her cheering squad at the finish line of life. She was about to experience her greatest win. The losing team was us.

I sat on the edge of her bed and eternity itself, gently rubbing her legs. How many times had she been in this position, singing

Pennies from Heaven or *The Three Little Fishes* while putting me to sleep as a little girl?

Shallow breaths intensified the atmosphere as we wondered if each one was her last. My heart danced between wanting her released from this world and all the pain consuming her fragile body, to a slight hope that she would sit up, start talking, and live with us a while longer. An ash color formed in her fingers and toes and ever so slowly traveled up her limbs . . . mottling they call it. Time was very short. Grandma's body was turning off. This was the final goodbye.

I had said everything I needed to say, but surprisingly even to me I blurted out, "I'll carry on!"

Grandma's legacy would live on in me. Her life and mine were grafted together through the divine web of faith, a purpose that far exceeded the family bonds of grandmother and granddaughter. Grandma breathed her last breath as a family friend walked in on cue singing *"Holy ground, we're standing on holy ground and I know that there are angels all around."*

It was holy, sweet, and incredibly sad.

Years later my Aunt Becky did find the scripture grandma had searched for the night Jesus' suffering gave her the strength she needed to face her own death.

> *"I am the Living One; I was dead, and now look,*
> *I am alive forever and ever!*
> *I hold the keys of death and Hades."*
>
> —Revelation 1:18 NIV

My Heart's Letter to Heaven

Grandma, if I could have one more chat with you we would have so much to catch up on. I know you saw the distant land of freedom in my heart. I walked towards it, but Grandma, I stopped.

Your story is teaching me and reaching me even now. The strength you showed in your death made you so beautiful. You embraced cancer with grace, dignity, and faith. You set the best example as you looked your earthly death straight in the face, took up your cross, and followed Jesus.

Thank you, Grandma. Thank you for not giving up on life and love after that heartbreaking train ride. I'm so sorry that happened to you. Thank you for deciding to make Jesus your Savior the day the kind man tapped on your front door. Thank you for carrying on in faith even though you never knew the complete and absolute treasure that you always were. I know you know it now.

Grandma, if you were here I would tell you are the most beautiful woman I've ever known. The Bible tells me, I am surrounded by a great cloud of witnesses; that includes YOU! I miss you so much, but I am learning that the same Spirit that lived inside of you lives in me too. I am throwing off things that easily tangle me up. I am running my race and fixing my eyes on Jesus. His Spirit is guiding me. I know The Truth. No more apologies. No more feeling like a burden. No more believing, I'm too much or I'm not enough. The effects of the train ride end here and, Grandma, your book is being written. Your story compels me forward. I will follow your example of faith. I got stuck, but I'm not staying stuck. I'm taking up my cross, I'm on my way. I'll see you soon.

Chapter 10

Mission and Purpose

Remembering Grandma gave me motivation to get back up again. I desired to take up my cross even though I wasn't quite sure how or exactly what that meant. I knew Jesus said in the Bible that if we wanted to follow him we must deny ourselves and take up our cross. The cross was the tool of execution where Jesus died. Did Jesus want me dead? *What does taking up your cross mean, Lord? I need clarification.*

Motivation to Get up and Keep Going

"Mama, is it easy to be a single mom with three children?" My youngest son, Trey, asked me in the midst of it all. Trey was an old soul from the get-go. He studied people and circumstances happening around him. The whole world was his classroom.

"No, Buddy, it's not."

"Well you make it look really easy, Mama."

AND SO SOMEHOW

Heaven's encouragement spilled out of his little voice. Those boys were the fuel that kept me in the game and off the bathroom floor, moving forward on a path of mustard-seed faith and hope.

Beyond Grandma's example, little-boy hearts filled with love, and the support of family, the Lord provided authentic friends who stayed with me through thick and thin. They were there when I was on a fast track of healing and when I had lain down as a victim and wallowed in my own despair. They are the type of friends who tell you when you have something in your teeth, when the outfit does make you look fat, and when to get over yourself. On a sleepy Sunday afternoon, Maggie, one of those friends called.

"I need to tell you this and please don't take me wrong, but I really feel led to tell you that you need to stop focusing on yourself and do something nice for someone else."

Excuse me, what? Are you freaking kidding me? Are you even serious right now? How dare she! I screamed inside my head. She had no idea what it was like to be me. Her words escalated my blood pressure and my heart pounded.

Truth be told, she had earned the right to say every word. Maggie had been by my side morning after morning while we pounded the pavement on long runs having some of the best truth-telling church as the world woke up.

Interestingly enough, a woman who ran a home for children in Jamaica had come to our church earlier that day. There was a team forming to go there. As she spoke, the idea of going did float through my mind. It floated out as quickly as it floated in. It was not realistic for me to go out of the country on a mission trip to serve someone else; I was living as a single mom barely managing us.

My friend's words sank in. I took a leap of faith and called the trip coordinator. To my relief she informed me that the trip was full.

Whew! I was off the hook. I tried. It just wasn't meant to be.

"Keep your heart open. Something will come up," Maggie cheerfully responded when I let her know to try and get her off my back.

A few days later, the trip coordinator called back to let me know more spots had opened up and asked if I was still interested. Gulp! Hard swallow! Okay, God! "Yes!" I answered with no clue of how it would work out.

In my lie-exposing and overcoming fest, I went from believing that I could not run to training for a half marathon. I asked people to pledge an amount for each mile of my marathon to help pay for my mission trip. Generous friends and family supported my cause. Plans were underway. What would this "getting my mind off myself and thinking about someone else" trip be?

Beautiful Ashes

We landed on the little Island of Jamaica. It was an eye-opening drive as I sat stuffed like a sardine on piles of luggage in an overpopulated jalopy of a van. All-inclusive resorts and the shacks of poverty were showcased through the windshield. How could these two extremes exist within one view? No one could have prepared me for this kind of shock and awe during the steep ride over potholes and partially paved roads through extreme poverty and into the tropical forest to the children's home. We practically fell out of the van at the entrance and were met with an entourage of little ones. After tucking in and hugging little ones going to sleep without a mama and daddy I fell asleep in an exhausted emotional heap.

The emotion of holding babies in the home's nursery and acting as a human jungle gym, not to mention a community Kleenex to many little bundles of energy the night before made the familiar smell of coffee very welcoming the first morning at The Robin's Nest Children's Home.

I tightly gripped my coffee mug and rocked in a wooden chair as an organized chaos of children scattered routinely about. There was nothing organized or routine about my life at that moment. I was an observer outside of herself and looking at the greater picture of life and pain. How I could serve these little ones dancing about during my short stay on a mission to *do something nice for someone else?* How could these little ones dance in the midst of their circumstances?

I sipped and pondered quietly as a little uniformed child exited the commotion and knelt down in front of me. She held a damp, white cloth in her hand. Slowly, diligently, with meticulous back and forth motion, her tiny hand held the cloth and wiped my feet. She did not speak or look at me. She washed and washed. What was happening? No one told her to do this. None of the other children were doing this. They were jumping and running and playing with toys. They were eating breakfast and getting their hair combed. She was on the floor, kneeling before me, diligently washing my feet.

Everything hushed. The world faded away. It was only this little one and me. She tenderly wiped my feet over and over and over as if she was compelled to do so. Heaven came to earth through tiny hands on my feet. Holy spilled in. I was being washed. Time stood still. Tears rolled down my cheeks. I would never be the same.

As quick as she had knelt down she popped back up and pranced away to find her place in the preschool line up and go master her ABC's. Overcome would be an understatement.

I came to serve. I came to do something nice for someone and get over myself and a preschool-schooler living in a children's home just washed my feet. She didn't know the blow to my heart that left me feeling lifeless and limp and how I was attempting to get life back. She knew nothing about the two years of pain that had led me here. I brought the medicine in my suitcase to help her and I just received a healing remedy from her that two years of counseling couldn't touch.

I learned that her name was Zoe, which means life. How fitting.

The next day this little foot washer and I met up on the playground. We swung together without care. As different as our lives and the reasons that led each of us to be at *The Nest* were, we had one strong thing in common: the one who knows and heals pain. We were both the least of these and everything to Him. *Maybe deep wounds can heal*, I thought. Ashes can be beautiful. What would He do with mine?

Chapter 11

Forward and Back Again

My dear friend, the one who put the M in the JLM club, our little girl gang from the 80's that eventually reunited, just went through months of chemotherapy treatments. She recently had both breasts removed. After surgery she found out that on top of five weeks of radiation and needing to live away from home to get the specific kind she needs, she will undergo another 42 weeks of chemo as well. Her faith is beyond anything I could put into words. (Maybe we will write a book together and get it to you one day.)

JLM has a continuous group chat. We update and encourage each other and the L and M send messages that keep us laughing. I humbled down and asked for prayer to focus and be able to finish this book. Missy wrote back, "Pour into that book like today is your last day." She has been given such a clear perspective in this season of her life. Coming from her made writing this part crystal clear. Where instincts would have me pretty it up and make you smile, I will tell the truth. And the truth is, after a very long separation with my husband, we divorced.

Divorced

This is where I could play the blame game. Blame my former husband, I mean *HE* was the one who had the affair right?! Blame myself—I was not an innocent by-stander. I could blame the example I had, childhood wounds, stress, and pressure. I could blame others. And I did. I went through the *whole* list. I came to the conclusion that placing blame was the perfect answer.

> *Your hand-to-hand combat is not with human beings, but with the highest principalities and authorities operating in rebellion under the heavenly realms. For they are a powerful class of demon-gods and evil spirits that hold this dark world in bondage.*
> —Ephesians 6:12 TPT

> *Watch out for your great enemy, the devil. He prowls around like a roaring lion, looking for someone to devour.*
> —1 Peter 5:8 NLT

The devil was one of the most beautiful angels God created. Even still, he was not content. He desired to be God. He fell from Heaven because of pride. (Thus the saying, *pride comes*

FORWARD AND BACK AGAIN

before the fall.) We are made in God's image. He loves deceiving humans because he is jealous of God's beauty that lives in us, through us, and is on us as image bearers of God. He wants us to turn away from worshiping God to worshiping him. His aim is to steal, kill, and destroy us.

The book of John says the devil is the Father of Lies. Lying is his native language. The devil has been lying to and deceiving humans since the beginning and he didn't stop with my life or my family.

I place credit where credit is due. I blame the deceiver and his deception that wreaked havoc. Did I play a part? Absolutely. Did my former husband play a part? You bet. Did his mistress? Uh-huh. Did people and the past influence? Yep. Who played a part? We all did. Each person must take appropriate responsibility. We are not spiritual puppets; we are people with choice. A *yes* and *no* ability. When we choose poorly, there are consequences. But it starts with deception. We take the bait of deception. It leads to more. Soon we are not sure what is true and trustworthy. Here a tangled web of toxic thinking and skewed perceptions is weaved until we do not know *which way is up*. This is where the deceiver can wash his hands of us for the time being. His purpose is accomplished. We believe the deception and act on it freely—and we did.

God hates divorce. I learned why. He doesn't hate divorced people. He gave the provision for certain circumstances. This book is not about that. (I do not advocate for divorce. I would not wish it on anyone. Take your time; slow down and get wise counsel for as long as it takes if you are considering divorce.) He hates what it does to people that he dearly loves. The research proves His position.

- Life expectancy for divorced people is significantly lower than for married people.
- The health consequences of divorce are so severe that a Yale researcher concluded "being divorced and a non-smoker is slightly less dangerous than smoking a pack a day and staying married."
- After a cancer diagnosis, married people are most likely to recover, divorced are least likely to recover.
- Men and women both suffer a decline in mental health following divorce, but research has found that women are more greatly affected.
- Mental health impacts of divorce include depression, hostility, difficulty with self-acceptance, personal growth, and positive relations with others.
- For a child, divorce shatters basic safety and the belief concerning their parents' abilities to care for them and to make decisions that truly consider their well-being. Research comparing children of divorced parents to children with married parents shows that children of divorce:
    > Are more likely to suffer academically, experience behavioral problems, and are less likely to graduate from high school.
    > Are almost five times more likely to live in poverty.
    > Are more likely to engage in drugs and alcohol.
    > Experience illness more frequently and recover from sickness more slowly.
    > Are more likely to suffer abuse.
    > Suffer more frequently from symptoms of psychological distress.

> Have emotional scars from the divorce that last into adulthood.[3]

I didn't know about the research then. I didn't need to. My heart felt it. My eyes saw it. It shaded our sunniest days. We all became statistical overcomers of so much. Even still, divorce is an earthquake with aftershocks that continue long after the papers are signed.

Remarried

A few short days before our divorce was to be finalized, my still aching and oh-so-not-ready heart went on a date. Aaron was a farmer of Dutch descent who captured my heart with his steady and stable predictability along with his sweet kids—a son and a daughter. He was a quiet Iowa farm boy who was dependable, trustworthy, and secure. He did what he said. His handshake could be trusted. I captured his heart with my passion, vision, and emotions. We quickly married.

Upon uniting our households, our unspoken blended family plan was doing activities together. Maybe if we did enough together we would melt two families into one. There are over 27,000 pictures on my computer documenting our best try at this *Blending the Fam* plan.

We did a lot and experienced a ton. You name it, we did it: from weekend camping and boating, to mission trips and vacations, restaurants, shopping, museums, concerts, conferences, movies, amusement parks and fairs, playing hide and

---

[3] AMY DESAI, J.D.. January 1, 2007. *How Could divorce Affect My Kids?*. www.focusonthefamily.com

seek, homemade zip-lines, paintballing, bonfires, snowmobiling, four wheeling, bouncing on a trampoline, and building snow forts on our farm. We celebrated holidays and birthdays and everything in between. We got involved in school, church, and community events. We hung out with family and friends and loved our neighbors near and far. We worked hard together at the little restaurant we purchased, the ground we farmed, and the mowing operation we started. We had fun and made a lot of memories, but no matter what we did or how much fun we had there was an underlying discord. The blended family itself was a constant reminder of the loss in our hearts. Nothing could remove it. Not time. Not fun experiences. Nothing could take it away.

My husband and I had conflicting ideas of how to eliminate this discord. A battle developed between us. My mantra was, *The kids are hurting, we need help!* I saw their wounded hearts and felt helpless to know what to do. Licking my own wounds was a full time job. How could I repair the earthquakes of life they all had endured? I thought of every scenario I could to get us all out of pain over and over like a dog chasing its tail. No matter what scenario I played out, the outcome remained the same: somebody was still hurting.

Aaron stayed in the camp of, *We just need to love each other and be one!* His thought was that love had to come from the top down. Showing affection to him with our kids around made me feel like we were inflicting more pain on them. We loaded cannons and shot arrows in the name of our battle cries: *Help the kids! Become One!*

One year into our marriage I was sure that I had made a grave mistake. In desperation we paid a visit to our pastor. He gave us a personality test to help us understand each other. The results were astounding. We are so opposite that when our pastor went over the results he exclaimed, "In all my years of marriage counseling, I have never met a couple as opposite as you! You might make it."

We MIGHT make it?! We came for hope and got a dose of reality. Still, it felt like winning the lottery as we processed through my passion and his quiet design and how to navigate the image of God weaved into our makeup. It was a step in the right direction, but running was still my instinctive remedy for pain relief; however, I was exhausted. I barely functioned when my boys were with their dad. Subconsciously, I devised a plan to get my husband to leave me. He would be the one to run away. I spoke every reason why we should not be together, stated my case, begged him to leave me and concocted passion-filled, award winning speeches as to why we should never be together, even quoting scripture and his own words back to him. His response remained the same after every try, "You can leave if you need to leave, but I love you and I am not leaving." This worn-out, one-sentence response infuriated me. I was a girl who knew how to throw fits and get her way. He continued with annoying predictability. The steady and secure man that captured my heart was now stubborn and refusing to leave. He stayed consistent, not caving to my victim mentality or coddling my demanding emotions. He did not try to save or rescue me. He refused to buy into the lies that shame screamed viciously at me. He spoke the truth in love. He stayed when I begged him to leave. I had met my match. He saw the worst of me and did not move. His will was stronger than mine. Strangely, it felt safe.

I lived in the tension of wanting to bolt and staying anyway. Something deep under the iceberg of me broke off. It ever so slowly floated to the surface while a life of broken *joy* and faith in God continued.

Another Mission Trip

My encounter with Zoe's foot washing stayed with me through the years and caused me to live differently a little more all the time as my husband and I wrestled with what it really meant to follow Jesus and live it out. This caused us to become uncomfortable. It made others around us uncomfortable too. Some ridiculed our ideas of sacrificing to help others or doing radical things to share the love of Jesus. It didn't stop us.

We led a few mission trips to the Robin's Nest and dreamed of farming and going overseas to do mission work between harvest and planting seasons. Our whole family agreed on adoption and completed the home study process with excitement. Books like *Crazy Love* by Francis Chan, *Radical* by David Platt, and *Kisses from Katie* by Katie Davis became my crash-course education into living out Maggie's tried and true advice to get my mind off myself and serve others.

At an inspirational speaking event, I was challenged to ask someone what their dream was and make it come true. My son, Collin, came to mind. I expected his answer to be a new snowmobile or something that went fast and had wheels. To my surprise he said, "I would buy the abandoned resort in Jamaica we saw when we were at the orphanage and turn it into a place where parents could come when they are adopting kids and where mission teams could stay."

I couldn't buy a million-dollar international property, but I could take him on a mission trip to Africa that he had been begging to go on with me.

We stuffed our suitcases with vitamins, medicine, medical supplies, formula, diapers, and clothing. Thirty-three Americans from around the country came together to visit orphans and support long-term missions on the ground in Africa. Our trip coordinators attempted to prepare us, but there were heartbreaks and miracles that no planning could have made me ready for.

Chapter 12

Miracles in Africa

I walked the uneven terrain to her African home. I've seen ones like *her* before on giant screens documented with impressive graphics as heart-tugging music played. *She's* been delivered in the mail alongside bills and credit card offers. Magazines have eloquently captured *her* and educated me on the fact that *she* lives on less than two dollars a day. I glanced at *her* when someone posted her on my news feed. Today it was different, I was at *her* doorstep. She was real, with a heartbeat, eyes that looked into mine, and a name: Vanessa.

Vanessa

Vanessa's father had died of AIDS and now her mother was preparing to do the same. Her siblings were sent away when her mother became too weak to care for them. Vanessa, *the strongest*, was chosen to stay and care for her dying mother.

When I saw ones like her in the past, I could click to another site, close the magazine, or toss the request in the trash. Not here. She was right in front of me. I trod in the ocean of poverty consuming Vanessa. My heart bled at the complexity of her life and the smallness of mine to fix anything for her for good. We gave her mother a bag of beans, flour, and a prayer. After hugging their thin bodies and preparing to leave, Vanessa held her hand out to me. I put it in mine, pulled her in close, and squeaked out, "Jesus loves you."

My heart broke. *Why are we here dropping off food that would be gone tomorrow and walking away? Why did you bring me to her doorstep God?* I asked, walking through the slums. *I sent you to Vanessa's doorstep today, I have been there all along. You touched her hand. I created it. You heard the heartbreak of her story. I died for her heartbreak. You are both fragile children with limits living in a fallen world. I am your strong Father who redeems and restores. I came to Vanessa's doorstep just as I came to yours. I have not forsaken you. I will not forsake her. Look higher, child. My ways are not your ways.*

With American distractions out of the way, God was clear. I saw him in the sheer joy of the African people who had nothing but lived as if they had everything. My soul was conflicted as I wrestled with the difference compared to life at home.

Healings in the Bush

On our way into the bush the next day, an open-air school feeding children food and knowledge while their mothers weaved baskets on the lawn welcomed us. Our team was split into groups. I was placed in the group delivering rice and beans. Single file, we shuffled through grass that resembled a tall Iowa cornfield in late summer as the mission base disappeared. The huts hidden in the bush came into view.

Exhaustion lived on the face of a mother who cared for her adult son with evil spirits tormenting him. We prayed. Her son glared. My mind attempted to grasp this desperate reality and how grateful she was for prayer and food. Where were the police, the mental health facilities, the self-help books, and the medication?

Once the rice and beans were gone, we went back to base. I sensed tension in the air. Desperate mamas had come and were lined up with their sick babies. Little ones spiked fevers of 104 and higher. It was a Malaria outbreak. The only medical professional was a nurse from the United States with few supplies and little training on African bush emergency protocols. He had arrived just a few weeks earlier to serve and love. This was his opportunity. Patient rooms were shade trees. Medicine was syringes filled with murky sugar water. A mother handed me her baby. Our eyes met. Her dire look spoke a mama-bear language that did not require an interpreter. *Please help!* they pleaded. Instinct kicked in. Thankfully, I had dressed in layers. I took off my top layer, dipped it in the dirty water, rung it out, and gently rubbed the forehead of the lethargic baby in my arms.

It felt like I had been cast as a cheap stand-in to a play with a plot that I didn't understand. At home I would have *all. the. things:* electrolyte fluids, medicine, doctors and nurses, a comfy rocking chair, clean water, and air conditioning. All I had was dirty sugar water in a syringe and the shirt off my back.

Jesus help! I prayed inside. *Say my name.* He answered. I put my hand on the baby's head cradled in my arms and whispered, "Jesus."

I did have something else—the name of Jesus. The name above every other name. I believed in the power of Jesus' name even though my Western life usually didn't display it as a first option. My Western methods were nowhere to be found. Jesus' name was readily available. (Oh how I would need that readily available name for what was to come.)

I prayed. The nurse took the baby's temperature. It was dropping!

Help! We need help over here!

I handed the baby back to his mama and communicated through a smile that her baby was improving and ran over to my friend calling for help.

"I don't think she's going to make it!"

A little girl was convulsing and foaming at the mouth as the blistering sun beat on her. Her eyes rolled back in her head and her thin body shook like a shutter in a windstorm. Her stiff body was riddled with fever. Her protruded belly and swollen feet imbedded with mites showed that crisis was daily life. The sun beat down on her. Adrenaline rushed in me, "Let's move her to the shade."

A handful of *unschooled and ordinary* Americans carefully carried her to the trunk of a tree.

"We need to pray." I declared.

Strangers just a week ago, we let go of any perceptions of strength and took hold of the powerful name of Jesus while we laid hands on the girl's trembling body.

Jesus! propelled out of our mouths. We asked him to heal this little girl hanging on to life by a thread. He did. She stopped trembling. Her eyes stopped rolling backwards. She sat up, opened her eyes, and spoke!

We need a translator! An interpreter ran over to our makeshift emergency room.

She said she needs to go behind the barn. Which meant she needed to go to the bathroom. She stood up and peed all over me. I had never been so glad to be peed on in all my life. I had just witnessed the power of Jesus heal this sick girl!

She went back to school to eat lunch. Every sick baby's fever dropped to normal at the name of Jesus that day! The mamas gathered them up with eyes that spoke a relieving *thank you* and they disappeared back into the bush. It wasn't a cheap play and I wasn't a stand-in. It was resurrection power. I wanted to be a main character in any scene of resurrection that followed.

Not the Same

After two weeks of rice and beans my clothes were getting loose; so was my grasp on my life back in America.

Aaron, Mom, and Grandpa Bob met Collin and me at the airport when we landed on the Fourth of July dressed in red, white, and blue with hand-held flags waving. The entire plane ride home, all I wanted was to hug my husband and eat a steak. When my feet hit American soil, I was discombobulated. My family grinned ear to ear to see their family home safe. My smile and hugs were half-hearted as two worlds crashed within me.

We drove to the nearest steakhouse. I ordered that steak I had been craving. While we waited I watched the food and drinks flow in abundance. The restaurant got annoyingly loud. Glasses clinking. Silverware tapping on plates. Surface chatter. TVs blaring. People laughing. The noise mismatched the continuous snapshots of the past two weeks that were spinning through my mind. My steak came. I could not eat more than two bites.

The consumerist ways of my world repulsed me. Still they were all I knew. How could life be so incredibly different for humans living on the same planet? I didn't have the answer. I did have more passion to follow Jesus every time I remembered Africa.

We sold our acreage and purchased a less expensive home to be positioned to give and go more. It had been a stressful couple of weeks between purchasing the new home and closing on our current one. Right before closing day on the acreage, the dishwasher in our kitchen malfunctioned and flooded two rooms. The new home was an old Victorian that needed a few renovations before we moved. Two houses were in disarray. Everything seemed to be coming all at once—but that was nothing compared to the devastating phone call when our physician's number lit up on my phone.

Not Prepared for This

For a few weeks my son Collin had repeatedly complained of a headache and being light headed. I knew it was real. He is not a complainer, but was unconcerned with anything of severity. I scheduled an appointment and took him to the doctor without worry. *Maybe it was a virus or something to do with the speed at which he was growing,* I thought. Our doctor took it seriously; he did a series of tests on his heart and scheduled an MRI of his brain. I was truly thankful for his thoroughness; it would reassure us it was nothing once we received the results. This was that sigh-of-relief call; I was sure of it.

Collin's physician was the next-generation doctor that followed his father, who delivered Logan and also Grandma's cancer diagnosis. Our boys were friends. His voice was familiar but seemed foreign as he spoke Collin's test results. The whole world disappeared in a muffled blur hearing the words *pediatric neurosurgeon and brain surgery* that highlighted his sentences. What I could not comprehend I jotted on paper that sat ready for service in the console cup holder of my minivan. Was this a sick April Fools' joke in October? Moments before, my priority was scraping layers of wallpaper off our soon-to-be kitchen walls and drying out carpets. In one phone call our whole world turned upside down.

Collin was diagnosed with severe Chiari malformation, a condition where the brain slips out of the skull. *No, No, No, not my boy!* Where is the playbook on how to tell your 15-year-old he has to have brain surgery? I mustered up strength to present as a strong confident and calm mama on the outside while feeling like a leaf blowing in a hurricane inside. I tripped over my words and broke the news as uncontrollable tears cascaded down his cheeks.

I have never been so eager to get to a doctor's office. The pediatric neurologist walked into the exam room. His presence caused us to rise to attention. He performed a series of neurological tests. Collin's gag reflex was almost non-existent. The tap on his knee to get a jerk reaction produced nothing. The images of his brain were lit up to explain why. His brain was 2 centimeters below his skull. The protective bone was squeezing his brain. Surgery was critical. A date was set. We went home to wait some more.

"Mom, what if I die? What if I wake up and I don't know you?" Collin asked. Talking about feelings isn't his jam; he's one who cuts to the chase. His question headlined all that was going on inside. Again, where is the playbook? Can someone please give it to me NOW!?

God will be faithful. No matter what. You will be okay. I will know you and love you, your family will be by your side. You will not be alone. I attempted to say with reassuring confidence.

Tears came. I hugged my scared boy. He got up and went to school as if life was normal. Nothing was normal. I wanted to take this from him or take him far away from this. I went into my bedroom, laid on the floor and wept violently.

What do you want? The calming voice of the Holy Spirit spoke.

What do I want? **I want my son to be well!**

As soon as my frustrated words of anger met the air, my heart repositioned.

And even more than that, I want your will. We will praise you in suffering, in medical or miraculous intervention, even if it means my son transferring to Heaven. Whatever brings you glory is what is best for my boy. That is what I want, my heart spoke. Peace rushed in and made itself at home. I lifted my head out of the teary bedroom carpet and got up to face the un-normal.

Peace leased its stately presence on the fourth-floor waiting room at the University of Iowa Hospital on surgery day a few weeks later. There was no blended, step, or exes there: just family. One team, wearing the same jerseys, running to the same goal. We laid hands on Collin and called on the name of Jesus just like I had done in the African bush.

Laughter lifted the heaviness during surgery prep, but the time came to hug Collin and walk out. I met eyes with the nurse. I communicated without words, *please help my baby*—as the African mamas had with me in the bush—and walked out. Sufficient grace flooded in. There would be one outcome. No matter what, Collin would have life. I didn't know what kind or how, but I knew he would.

To our surprise the surgery was completed in nearly half the predicted time. The doctor came into the consultation room, giddy, like a kid in a candy store. Was this the same doctor that we stood at attention to weeks earlier? He flew around the world teaching other doctors his expertise and played his prominent position well. Not today. He flung the images of Collin's brain on the light board like confetti. *"I made the first couple of incisions and his brain "just floated up." It was much less invasive than I expected!"* The hand of God touched my son's brain and *floated it up*; now I was the giddy one!

Collin's question popped back into my head as I walked to see him in recovery, *Mom what if I don't know you?* Panic shot through my giddiness. This was the moment of truth. I took hold of Collin's hand to let him know I was there. His dad did the same on the other side of the hospital bed. We let him know the surgery was over, and he was okay. Tears streamed down his cheeks. His hands squeezed ours tight. There was a long road of recovery ahead but our son would be well.

Chapter 13

A Formal Invitation Into Suffering

"Mom you've got to learn about sex trafficking!" was the plea of Logan's voice on the other end of the phone. *What trafficking?* I didn't even know what that meant. I had heard of human trafficking and I felt sorry for people in third-world countries that had to work long hours, but what was a small town girl from Iowa supposed to do about that?

The soft-skinned little boy that made me a teen mom was now a young man learning about himself and the world. Logan is someone who, when he gets drummed up about something... well, watch out. His heart of justice is a roaring lion. He viewed a video, *Nefarious: Merchant of Souls*. It showcased sex trafficking happening in countries all over the world including the U.S. He did what any smart young man would do: purchased the video, brought it home, and got it in front of his mama bear saying, "Mom, please watch this when my little brothers are not around." I was shocked with what I saw. Slavery hadn't ended. There are over 27 million slaves in the world. Inside that desensitizing number are little girls and boys in their most formative years being sold repeatedly by others for the profit of someone else. Men and women, sold 10–20 times a day for sex by pimps who control them with physical force, mental fear, intimidation, and the promise of dreams that will never come true. They can be beaten, isolated from society, threatened that the ones they love will be killed if they do not submit, brainwashed, addicted to drugs, or even forced to recruit others into this world. Victims of this hideous crime live through unspeakable trauma day after day while someone gets rich off of what their body can offer someone who is willing to pay the price. My heart broke in a way it had not been broken. I wept for faces I had never seen and hearts whose stories I didn't know. I grieved for little ones who had everything stolen from them. I ached for innocent skin that selfishness continually touched. I laid my head on my pillow, but sleep would not come. Each time my eyes closed I saw a little girl in a dark room in my mind's eye. The door to the room opened; a dark presence overwhelmed her. The door opened again. The dark presence left. It happened over and over. She was screaming but it was silent. No one heard her. No one came. She was small, trapped, and helpless.

I am not typically one to be angry at God and blame him for the tragedies that humans choose to do to each other out of their own free will. Sex trafficking of innocent children put me over the edge. *Why God? I don't understand?* I got up, prayed, researched sex trafficking, and emotionally posted on Facebook.

A FORMAL INVITATION INTO SUFFERING

At this point, I had been camped out in Philippians 3:10,11 the verse I had heard in the cold of winter inside my warm minivan so many years ago.

> *I want to know Christ and the power of his resurrection. To share in the fellowship of suffering, becoming like him in his death and so somehow to attain resurrection from the dead.*
>
> —Philippians 3:10,11 NIV (paraphrased)

I want to know Christ and the power of his resurrection was my heart's cry. I had prayed the first two phrases of Philippians 3:10 over and over for years. Know Christ. Know resurrection. I had not prayed the third phrase, *to share in the fellowship of suffering*.

Sex trafficking was an invitation into suffering. I was invited. Ugh! Who wants to be on the A list of a suffering event? I'm guessing not you. Certainly not me, a girl who knows how to smile and pretty it up.

My Philippians 3:10 prayer was being answered in the most peculiar way. It was as if the Lord was saying, *Joy, you want to know me? You want to know my heart? Come and see what was on my mind when I was on the cross. Know what I was dying for. Understand why the cross was so bloody and traumatic. Come into my heart and see the violence that was overcome. Take up your cross. Follow me. Know my precious daughters by name. Hear their weeps, see their wounds, and bear witness to their pain.*

I knew Jesus died on the cross to pay for sin. He was leading me into more.

The Cross, where Jesus went into suffering and touched it. Everything. All of it. Abuse, victimization, addiction, sickness, divorce, acts of selfishness, wrong perceptions, distorted thoughts, fear, lies, death, grief, pain, abandonment, isolation, manipulation, torture, destruction, murder, hatred, hypocrisy, falseness, and every shred of divisiveness and deceit that has ever or will ever occur for every human from the beginning until the end. Jesus touched suffering and bore it all as if it was his own. He wore it on his own body, and was beaten until he was unrecognizable. He paid for what we did and what was done to us that caused a separation from perfect communion with God, ourself, and others: a debt he didn't owe. He came into our suffering so that we were not alone in it. He made a way through and paved a way out of suffering for us as God's wrath poured out on him. He got what we deserved. What looked like death was producing life. Jesus defeated sin, death, and hell through sacrificial love. He made a public spectacle out of the devil as he hung in humility, barely breathing.

God was intimately inviting me into suffering with Him. That night I had a decision to make. I could cry, feel the big emotions, and in days this would all fade away, *or* I could accept the invitation.

It didn't all come together that night but there was a shift in my spirit. I traded my dream of overseas missions and adoption for his call to the issue of sex trafficking.

Grandma's Ring

I knew the first step, but my heart ached as I took Grandma's ring into the local jewelers. She gave it to me shortly before she died. It was a gold nugget ring she had designed with the diamonds out of Grandpa's wedding ring after his ring finger was taken off during a farming accident. Wearing it was like having a part of her and grandpa with me every day. People needed to know about sex trafficking, and I knew that whatever grandma's ring was worth, it needed to be the money used to purchase the rights to show the movie *Nefarious: Merchant of Souls* to others. Grandma would agree from Heaven's viewpoint no matter how much she loved jewelry while she was here.

The first miracle happened the day I picked up the proceeds. The jeweler handed me the exact amount of cash needed to purchase the rights to the film and then a tiny plastic bag with three diamonds in it.

"These aren't worth anything," he said.

My heart exploded. Maybe to the rest of the world these had no value, but to me those diamonds were pure gold. I still had the most precious parts of the ring. I tucked them safely away. Someday I would have a ring made for each woman God provided for my sons. Grandma's legacy would literally carry on in those tiny stones and the melted gold that would educate the world on sex trafficking.

My husband and I, along with a few others, showed the movie in two theaters in Iowa. From there, 12 people came together in a movement of prayer and asked God, *What do you want us to do about 27 million slaves in the world?*

Prayer turned into education, research, and talking to people who were smarter and wiser than we were. How would a group of grass roots, *modern-day net droppers* make a dent in the second-largest criminal industry in the world?

The anti-trafficking movement was growing. Prevention, law changes, stopping the demand, awareness, recovery, and restorative aftercare to survivors were the lanes of help people were getting into. A mathematical equation showed us our lane would be restoration. According to the Urban Institute Study of 2012, hundreds of thousands of people were being sold for sex every year, yet there were only a fraction of beds in the United States designated to the aftercare of sex trafficking survivors. There was a need.[4]

The complexity was overwhelming. There was no one way people's lives ended up in sex trafficking but there were commonalities. Most lives trapped in this hell had traumatic beginnings. Often their family was unsafe; many sifted through the foster care system, and were easily lured in after family and systems failed. Trafficking commenced in childhood, and victims crossed the line into adulthood while living this hideous life. If they were able to get out, where would they go? It was possible for a survivor to have no documents of identification, no high school education, and have never had a normal job in her life. People had used and abused her; who could she trust? How would she function "normally" after potentially hundreds or thousands of people had exploited her for years—or even all of her life—if she did get out?

Wings of Refuge

Through prayer, research, and education the Lord showed us that our way of serving survivors would be to provide a safe place to land; this landing place would be a home known as Wings of Refuge. Steps were completed to form a nonprofit while we continued to educate ourselves and others. We met with anyone who was willing. Some thought it was a pipe dream that would fade away, others wished us well, some vetted us out

---

4 "Report: Investigation and Prosecution of State and Local Human Trafficking Cases," Urban Institute, Northeastern University, April 2012, https://www.ojp.gov/pdffiles1/nij/grants/238795.pdf.

A FORMAL INVITATION INTO SUFFERING

(with good reason), and a few thought we were crazy but didn't tell us until later. Many joined us and we surged forward.

Meeting with individuals and groups around the state became a full-time job. One afternoon I sat in a local coffee shop sharing the mission with two therapists. They offered insight to supporting survivors of intense trauma. I took notes and chewed on every word. Their mouths exploded with wisdom. Towards the end of our meeting, they agreed to counsel women once we were up and running. I was elated. As our time came to a close, I snuck in one more question for these trauma gurus.

What do you think about repressed memories? Have you ever worked with anyone who had repressed memories or do you think it's a hoax?

Seeing *those kinds of people* on TV talk shows that got the ratings made me want to puke. I knew repressed memory was a dramatic attempt to get attention by over-the-top drama seekers but needed confirmation from the experts.

"We see it all the time," the therapist responded in her thick Ethiopian accent. And then she looked straight into my being and without skipping a beat declared,

"Do not worry, if there is something to remember the Lord will reveal it to you when it is time. Stop trying to remember. People remember when they feel safe."

My face had to have been a dead giveaway to the shock of her words. How did she know I was asking for me? I had said nothing to her. Nothing. I didn't leak a clue in our meeting about the increasing dark flashes that woke me up, the constant alarm inside my brain that never stopped playing out worst-case scenarios, the fear and control that dictated my every moment, facts I was learning about my not-so-safe father, or how the more I was educated about indicators of sexual abuse, the more I realized my life was a textbook example of it. Was I a detective being given clues to crack a case, or a dramatic over-thinker? Hearing the therapist's divine words allowed me to go home and forget about thinking about if there was anything to remember. Probably there was nothing at all.

Wings of Refuge birthed through one miracle after another, which was awesome and hard. Even in the "hard" I knew this was the dream of my little-girl heart playing out in real time. I was speaking on stages, telling people about the problem of sex trafficking and Jesus who died and rose to overcome it. Like a laser of light, I walked on the straight path he was forming out of my crooked one. I didn't ask to go and speak; people reached out. I had no training as a public speaker; somehow I did it next to attorney generals, FBI agents, and other leaders in the anti-trafficking movement—with knees knocking and voice cracking. I spoke to anyone who asked and anyone who would listen. When people found out that slavery hadn't ended and all over the world people were being sold every day for someone else's profit, they got on board and gave money, prayer, encouragement, time, and talent. Passion burned inside me like a fire. The famous quote of missionary, C.T. Studd, became a reality in my daily life. *Some wish to live inside the sound of church and chapel bell, I wish to run a rescue shop within a yard of hell.* Wings of Refuge would be just that, a rescue shop for the ones God plucked out of this *hell*. As you can imagine, hell does not like rescue shops set up at all, let alone within a yard of sex trafficking. *Wings* would be a place where young women could come to know they are valued, have hope, and are loved by Jesus. Wings answered our question, *What does it mean to follow Jesus with our lives?* It was the obedience of taking up my cross, letting go of my plan of overseas missions and adoption, and following Jesus. Hell hated it.

Chapter 14

The Other Side of the Door

God's word says that light shines in the darkness and the darkness cannot overcome it. His light was shining bright on the dark crime of sex trafficking through the ministry of Wings of Refuge. The 12 of us were being awakened in the Spirit and our eyes were wide open.

At this point I was learning to draw healthy boundaries with Mom that codependency had erased. It was not my responsibility to make Mom happy. I was not an extension of her. I was my own person with rights and responsibilities. This felt like betrayal. The more freedom and clarity I had, the more difficult our relationship became.

One afternoon after a frustrating conversation with Mom that left me feeling anguished, I laid on my living room floor crying and asking the Lord the question I had been wrestling with for years that left me feeling shame, guilt and condemnation each time I thought about it. *Why can't I honor my mother and father? What is wrong with me? I have a calling on your life. You need to stop living as a small, trapped, helpless little girl.* His statement seemed random for the moment at hand, until he took me into a vision. I knew by now he was a supernatural God—beyond the tangible, beyond my own understanding, and I freely let my spirit connect with Him as He unfolded this vision in the supernatural realm.

I saw a white door with a golden knob. The door was so tall that I couldn't see the top. The door terrified me.

No. No. No! I was terrified to see what was on the other side.

Trust me. He had proven himself over and over and over. I could trust Him, no matter what was on the other side of the door.

Jesus lovingly took my hand and put it on the knob with his. Together we turned it. The door cracked open. Light, like that which people describe in near-death experiences, poured out from the other side and propelled the door wide open. The indescribable light exploded and burst out. It flooded me and the whole room as I lay face down on my living room floor. It was breathtaking. There are not adequate words to describe the beauty that exists in His light. The words of the old hymn "and the things of earth grow strangely dim in the light of his Glory and grace" made perfect sense.

It was more than light; it was the deepest love I have ever felt. It covered me like a warm blanket. It consumed my being at every level. I thought I was dying, yet I was 100% fine with it. It was amazing. I was the happiest I had ever been. I lay facedown in worship and awe. It was The Light of His Glory. I never wanted to leave. It encompassed me. Time was suspended. My soul was forever satisfied. I was not small, trapped, or helpless.

I was safe, complete, and whole. I had no need or want in His Glory. I was abandoned to the world and found in Him. If this is what forever was like, let it begin.

Without warning, while swooning in The Light it shifted. Jesus took the light of who He is, and placed it on the dark spot in me. I moaned a foreign sound. I wasn't even sure it was coming out of me. Where was it coming from? A groaning came out of my depths, a place I had never felt before. My body trembled. I shivered uncontrollably.

What my brain had separated off and protected me from knowing consciously almost my whole life was revealed. Jesus put his light on my dark spot. It was what he was slowly leading my receiving heart to on my bedroom floor each time I opened my heart and journal. Now was the time. He was right on time. Jesus walked me into the suffering of my stolen innocence. I saw the sexual harm I had suffered as a little girl: small, trapped, and completely helpless.

My husband came home from work. I wept and wept and wept in his secure and steady arms. I wept in a way I did not know humans could weep. I wonder if it was a weep like Joseph's in the Bible, when he was face to face with his brothers who sold him into slavery?

Because of jealousy, Joseph was left for dead and sold into slavery by his brothers. He was enslaved and imprisoned for years. He was eventually a slave to Pharaoh. Joseph had a gift of interpreting dreams and used it to aid Pharaoh. This eventually promoted him to second-in-command under Pharaoh. Joseph married, ruled Egypt with Pharaoh, and had two sons: Manasseh, meaning *God made me forget all my trouble and my father's house*, and Ephraim, meaning *God made me fruitful in my suffering*. His past was finally behind him. The names of his children were the billboard to prove it.

As was his role, Joseph interpreted a dream of Pharaoh's predicting a famine. Egypt stored up a surplus. When the famine hit, Joseph's brothers, who had left him for dead years ago, got hungry. His father ordered them to go to Egypt for food. When they did, they had to ask Joseph to give them food. It had been so long, they did not even recognize him. Joseph recognized them. He was face to face with his suffering. The trouble he had forgotten, and the past he had beaten, was now standing right in front of him begging for food in order to live. Joseph called for everyone to leave his presence. Once alone, he wept so loud that the Egyptians and all of Pharaoh's household heard him.

I wept like Joseph seeing the sexual abuse I had suffered as a child. God's glory exposed the root of my shame. The crime scene was revealed. Textbook identifiers were clues: the painfully shy and hideously angry child, the self-conscious middle schooler who gained control by what went into her mouth and the ability to purge it back up, the rebellious out-of-control teen that gave sex to be loved who became a teen mom. The 20-something young woman riddled with fear who tried to beat her own demon through perfection and control, and the 30-something broken woman who failed miserably at perfection that was now the present me bewildered at the security and safety in my husband. The case was solved. It all made sense with light on it.

Next Steps

Mom woke up and squeezed my hand tight. She adamantly repeated, "I didn't know. I didn't know!" I knew exactly what she was talking about. My heart wanted to tell her, *I know, Mom. The words would not come, even though I had already said them to her before.* She drifted back to sleep.

Mom's repeated statement to me in her final days went from, "I didn't know," to just *"know."* I had confronted my mom about my Father's sexual abuse. She went into hysterics. She was sad I got hurt and very worried about any blame being placed on her. "It's not my fault, I didn't know. I didn't abuse you. Don't be mad at me!"

Our relationship was never the same. I believed mom didn't actually know. But I needed her to be a mom, not the victim in need of consoling. I needed her to tell me it was going to be okay. I needed her to be the parent, rise up, and lead the way to healing, restoration, and forgiveness even though I was an adult. I knew there could be healing. It didn't have to be this way.

Relating to Joseph

Joseph wept loud but his story didn't end with weeping. The place that was supposed to take Joseph out became the place where he was positioned to save those who tried to take him out. He revealed himself to his brothers, saying, "I am Joseph, the one you sold into slavery."

Where Joseph could have taken revenge, he took up his cross. Where Joseph could have continued in disassociation and avoidance, he entered into his suffering and found his voice. "Don't be upset or angry with yourselves any longer because of what you did. You see God sent me here ahead of you to preserve life."

Joseph's fragmented heart became whole. God gave him the power to forgive. He embraced his brothers and kissed them one by one. Healing and forgiveness flowed into Joseph and his brothers. He moved his entire family to be close to him and the 12 tribes of Israel were established out of them. (Genesis 37–50)

God was calling me to bear the burdens of others, but first I needed to fellowship with Him in my own. The Lord placed me in front of small, trapped, and helpless little me from all those years ago. The warmth of His light melted me. I was no longer frozen and alone in that memory. All the disassociated parts of me that had separated off from God, myself and others could now begin to flow together and fellowship with the Lord there. Jesus, the Light of the World, lit up my whole world. I inched my way out of the wreckage of sexual abuse with Him, and step by step released the fears that had held me captive for so long.

Suffering and resurrection colliding was no joke. When the body gets safe, the heart remembers. In safety, the pain of the past surfaces, and needs to be processed in the present. Healing is not for the faint of heart. It's work: hard work. Many avoid it, push it down, and medicate with cream-filled pastries, a fifth of alcohol, a drug of choice—prescribed or off the street—or a life of perfection, performance, and success. I tried many of these faulty pain killers and landed on the hard truth that what happens in trauma is not the fault of the one hurt, but healing is still his or her responsibility. That reality just plain stinks.

Practically what that looked like was keeping my heart, journal, and bible open like a 24—hour diner and surrounding myself with supportive friends and family. I continued to learn about sexual trauma and how the Lord restores through others those who had been through it. I got my hands on every book or video I could. The core of healing was happening. The counselor with the thick Ethiopian accent who agreed to be the counselor for our restoration home first became mine.

My husband and I juggled healing, the whirlwind of being married to each other, raising teenagers in a blended family, running a restaurant, a farming and mowing operation, and the mission of Wings. I still gave overused speeches to my husband about how we were hurting our kids by being together. One night he gave me a different response than in the past:

"Why is what Jesus did on the cross good enough for everybody but you? We've all sinned and been sinned against. We can't go back and change it. There is nothing that is going to take away what has happened to our kids. Do you think the way you are thinking is helping them? Would it be helpful to live in the forgiveness that Jesus offers you and show our kids that?"

Tears filled my eyes. Forgiving others? OK. Forgiving myself? NEVER.

Chapter 15

The Hostage

I frantically rubbed the fibers of my jeans with one hand and clenched my overused Kleenex in the other. I was asked to describe out loud how I felt about my former self. It was like describing a hostage situation. I had myself gagged and bound inside. She was unforgivable. Worthy of nothing but the shame she felt. She deserved to be punished. She thought she was so pretty, skinny, and sexy. She thought she could actually attract a man, be loved, and feel secure. I knew the truth. I knew better. She was a fraud. She was the biggest poser I knew. She was not worth it. I blamed her. Everything was her fault: the divorce, the pain of her children and step-children, the misery of her husband now. She was pitiful and was getting what she deserved.

Two women trained to facilitate "negotiations" such as these through an inner healing process called *The Ultimate Journey* were advocating freedom for me. I wasn't afraid to let them know how bad she was. I hated her. No one could change my mind on that.

Wow. I don't see what you see. I see a strong woman who was put in an extremely difficult situation and had to deal with heartbreak. I see someone who didn't get what she needed and got a lot of what she didn't need. That's what I see, recanted the women leading me into the deep waters of the past.

My stubborn will held tight battling the rage between me, myself, and I as the negotiators did their best to free the hostage no-good woman.

Maybe that's it? Maybe she should stay where she is held hostage paying for everyone's mistakes and not be extended forgiveness? Maybe Christ's blood wasn't enough for her. Oh my word, here we go again! I thought.

Her sentence lingered in the silence like a banner waving over my head. The internal battle manifested externally as my leg uncontrollably bounced up and down. I tried to hold it still with the weight of my hands like it was a separate limb that didn't even belong to my body.

A rescue needed to happen. My head knew it. My heart fought it tooth and nail. I had a choice: stay stuck in un-forgiveness or let myself off the hook and walk out of the *hostage situation as a free* woman.

"Tell her what she needs to hear," one of the women challenged me.

I knew what she needed. I could give it to everyone else; not me, I needed to pay.

January 9, 2015 (Journal Entry/ Encounter with the Lord)

I skip over a lot of the Old Testament. God is angry and judges a lot. I like the New Testament. Jesus. Savior. Healer. Friend. God as Judge? No thanks.
You need a Judge. He who touched you touched the apple of my eye.
I say out loud a statement heard from another woman's testimony.
When he touched me, he touched the apple of God's eye.
I knew He cared. I didn't know it made God mad that I was touched in a way that repulses his heart. God is angry about it. There is vengeance in his heart. God is an avenger, a superhero who is right. I'm tired of avenging, seeking out my own forms of justice, attempting to right wrongs, living as if it all depends on me. My load is heavy with judgements for myself and others. I'm not managing well. Papers are falling out of this bursting caseload. Going a little deeper, I'm prideful. I think I know best. I can't give you this case because they hurt me too deeply. They need to pay. I can't give you mine; I should pay. I need to get better, do better, be better. I will try harder.
The Judge speaks. *Hand it over.*
His words shake me. I am Jell-O legged with my familiar case files in a tight hug at my chest. They seem foreign to hold standing before a Holy Judge. I hand them over. There is immediate release. God's judgment is good. It knocks down my invisible wall of self-protection. He builds a wall of right protection around me. I'm no longer a wide-open target. I have a just Judge. He decides. There is payment. It will come through God's judgment or Jesus' blood—not through me.

Forgiving the Hostage

The wrestle was beyond anything my soul had felt sitting in the small office with freedom's facilitators. They were midwives at my side helping me labor through the grueling birth pains. I was in the laboring phase where I wanted to call it quits. I wrestled so hard internally and let them know it but it was too late. We were too far along in the birthing process. The time was now: time for me to tell myself what I needed to hear. Through guttural sobs, I told myself, *It's not your fault. You were doing the best you could in the hardest place of your life. You would never intentionally hurt your boys. You love your boys and want the best for them. You would do anything you could to help them. You would not intentionally hurt anyone. You did the best you could in the biggest heartbreak of your life. I forgive you. You are free.*

I sided with God and took hold of what Jesus took hold for me on the cross. The cross became so intimate and personal: every whip, every lash, every jeer and humiliation, every drop of blood—for me. For all of me. The cross was not just for everyone else, it was specifically for me too. Resurrection is what I desired; forgiveness forged the way. I was given new eyes to see myself with a heart of compassion. Mercy's kiss rested on me. A breath of air resurrected truth. Sure, I played a part. I needed to take appropriate responsibility for myself, but forgiveness blew out the lie that it was *all* my fault. The fine wine of truth paired with the choice to believe it was poured in front of me. God knew it. Others saw it. I sipped it. It renewed my mind and filled empty places where lies had been gutted out but the renovation had never been complete. My head and heart connected in truth and love. I drank living water from the well of who He is and agreed with him as I did. I was not a very, very good little girl or a horrid girl, I was His girl. He did not create me a victim or a victimizer but a victor like Him. I lost a thousand pounds that day.

Chapter 16

On a Mission

He always comes alongside us to comfort us in every suffering so that we can come alongside those who are in any painful trial. We can bring them this same comfort that God has poured out upon us.

—2 Corinthians 1:4 TPT

At this point I was convinced that sex trafficking was a global, national and even a midwestern issue in places like Chicago, St. Louis, or Minneapolis. I wasn't convinced it was in Iowa.

Speaking was becoming routine. I arrived early, set up information, completed a mic check, and settled in the front row. Check. Check. Check. The list was complete. A young woman sat down beside me. Something was not right. She quickly cut to the chase: "*The reason I came tonight is because you are going to talk about my life.*"

It was like being at Vanessa's doorstep all over again. I had read books and watched movies about sex trafficking, attended conferences, visited websites, made phone calls, and learned from every expert I could, but I had never met a survivor in person. Here she was standing in front of me with glazed eyes and bandaged arms from cutting. She was proof. The ministry we were being called to was necessary in the midst of the *"Iowa Nice"* cornfields.

How I spoke that night with her in the room is still a mystery to me. Was every word triggering or freeing her? I was telling the storylines of her life as she sat and listened. When it was over, I beelined to the host who rallied her network for help. (This young woman did get help, received Jesus and is on a healing journey with him).

Meeting an Iowa survivor face-to-face gave our team confirmation we were headed on a needed mission. A phone call gave us drive to get the mission off the ground when a passionate woman spoke of an Iowa town with a juice bar that had opened its doors. The girls danced for patrons. When the bar closed they were sold for sex in hotels through the night. The town residents rolled up their sleeves and did what Iowan's do best-got to work. Whether in shorts and t-shirts on humid summer nights or long underwear and Carhart coveralls in the dead of Iowa winter, they protested the club and proclaimed a *you matter campaign* to the girls by building relationships with the girls, patrons, and the club owners. They provided necessities and gave flowers to the girls. They knew their campaign was worth it when a young woman let them know she wanted out and were given my contact information to help her.

My heart rate increased as I listened to the need for a place to go. We didn't have a home. We couldn't end anything for this woman. The Wings home needed to get open . . . soon!

By now our group was tightly knit together by a shared mission. Love flowed. Passion burned. We prayed and fasted over modern day slavery. We did all of the American things that must be done to form a non-profit *and* held our first planning retreat. Two outcomes came out of that. Our why: So exploitation ends for one more girl. Twenty-seven million was a number that could easily make you want to throw your hands up in the air and walk away. We might not wipe out slavery on the planet, but we could wipe it out for the one in front of us. The second outcome of our time at the cabin retreat was that we committed to saying yes to the next woman who called.

A few months later that call came.

It felt like I was going to see someone's new baby as my husband and I drove to meet the first survivor whose exploitation was ending at Wings of Refuge. Would she be terrified of us? What would she be like? What would the conversation sound like? Nervous excitement played Ring Around the Rosie in my heart.

Nothing turned out as I expected. Within minutes she had everyone in check. She was no stranger to strangers or awkward situations. She knew how to fake a smile and sell a dream. She was not a scared little girl in the corner like I imagined, at least not on the outside. She was a sassy and fast talking young woman with her doctorate in street smarts. She educated us. I'm not sure which miracle we were on by now, but she was a big one.

She traveled the country on *automatic* (meaning she traveled without her pimp and rolled money back to him.) She knew she needed to get out when she saw one of her *tricks* (customers) on the news wanted for murder. Bravely she drove herself to the police station and turned herself in for the many prostitution charges she had. She was safe in jail. In the coming months a series of events led her to Wings even though Wings was not yet a physical brick and mortar location. One of our board members who were empty nesters and former foster care parents became our first Wings of Refuge home. The rest of our team came together to offer hope and possibility on a daily basis to one more girl.

One year of living life with her rookie Wings family gave a safe and welcoming home with her own room, foundational counseling, a built up resume, and a savings account, but most of all a different perspective that there were people that didn't think about what they could get from her but thought about the good they wanted for her. She wore a cap and gown and ate a piece of her own graduation cake, something she thought was impossible. Most importantly, no one made a dime off of her body during her time at Wings. Exploitation ended for one more girl.

Wings literally had wings.

A family generously purchased a home to house three survivors at a time and rented it to Wings. Our Board of Directors calculated what it would take to run the home fully staffed for one year. Three weeks later on Christmas Eve, we received a call. A $250,000 gift was being given to Wings, the exact amount the board had decided but not told anyone about. Miracles and obstacles were everywhere.

When Wings of Refuge started, I was naive. I envisioned a happy little restoration factory where survivors would be like daughters and my husband would walk them down the aisle on their wedding day. The restoration cookie cutter would pop them out to go live happy lives. They would have children, a house with a white picket fence, drive minivans (update: crossover vehicles), and be soccer moms.

I learned Wings was not a factory. It was a bridge. There was a gaping canyon between a woman living inside the life of sex trafficking and being free from it. Wings bridged that gap with an opportunity to walk across the canyon and not fall into the abyss.

We were not called to *"restoration factory"* results, we were called to be faithful. There was no cookie-cutter approach or a one-size-fits-all. Freedom looked different for everyone. The victory of sleeping more at night, getting up and going to therapy one more time, graduating Wings and coming on staff to help others, or leaving Wings, and not involving yourself with trafficking initiatives ever again were all outcomes of freedom. Sometimes freedom—as crazy as it may sound—was the ability to choose to go back to the life of trafficking because love doesn't force you to stay. She was free to stay in and do the hard work of healing for as long as it took and as long as she was willing.

When the can of worms of sex trafficking was opened in my life, many people warned me I wouldn't want to see what I found. They were right. Beyond the hideous abuse and trauma, I began to see the breakdown in culture that encourages the outcome of sex trafficking:

- A devaluing of covenant marriage and family
- A deep deception on the earth targeting humans identity and worth
- A hook up culture where sex is nothing more than recreation and a marketing plan
- Pornography (aka *the gateway drug* to purchasing sex) rampant and socially accepted
- Consumerism that often values things over people
- The drug world and addiction that tightly holds the hand of sex trafficking
- Satanic tentacles that held women's souls and minds in bondage when their bodies did get free.

On top of all of this, sexual abuse was the common untold story everywhere I went. Whether in the souls at the Wings home, those who sat in church pews when I spoke, shook my hand at civic engagements, messaged me privately over social media, or asked to meet for coffee or in a quiet room in the church I was at because finally someone was like them.

Approximately one in three females and one in four males is the stat. Whether a teenage girl in foster care, a Christian home-schooled family member, or an elderly man telling his story through tears as his wife held his hand, numbers were people. If it took a village to raise a child, it would take an army to restore one. The *one* was everywhere.

Speaking was doing more than spreading awareness about sex trafficking. The light of His Glory was touching wounds of small, trapped, and helpless little hearts living in grown up bodies. The days before an event were a spiritual wrestling match . . . especially when I shared my testimony. Sometimes I wondered if it was worth it. Then I met Rachel.

That's her! That's her! I looked up to see two women looking straight at me on the other side of the booth. I was standing in a merchandise tent at an event with shoulder-to-shoulder people when the mother looking at me started her sentence, "You spoke in our town," and her daughter finished it, "And you saved my life."

I quickly shimmied my way through the ocean of people to hug the two ladies. Rachel and her mother shared her story in the crowded tent. Rachel was sexually assaulted on a college spring break trip. She tried to live as if it had never happened, but with no success. It burdened her to the point of wanting to take her own life. Before she did, she decided to visit her family one last time.

I spoke at her family's church the weekend she went home for her final visit. Spirit led words that I spoke in the little church that morning touched Rachel's buried deep wound. She fled the sanctuary and found an empty Sunday school room to let out her *Joseph weep*. Her mom followed.

"*Go get Daddy,*" she sobbed.

With her parents bearing witness to her suffering, she found her voice that day. She entered into the invitation of suffering with Jesus. God's light shined on her dark spot. She healed. It gave her passion to help others. "*Worth it,*" I thought.

Stories matter. God used my story to ignite healing in Rachel. Rachel's story fueled passion in me to continue even when it was hard. Your story matters, it could be the hope someone is waiting for.

One More Girl

Stories piled up in a worn-out turquoise folder in my briefcase. Inside were homemade cards, handwritten letters, emails, paintings, testimonies, pictures, and a funeral bulletin all from *one more girl*. I intentionally toted them around to remind me why it was important to share my story and the story of Wings, even though it was hard. One day it hit me, *I carried her story*. Stories that could be a book within themselves were carried in my folder and in my heart.

God confirmed the word he spoke to my heart about Logan being a key He would use for many to know Him through the beautiful chaos of stories unfolding at Wings. Logan's passion to get the information about sex trafficking in front of his mama bear was what the Lord used to change many lives.

Stories of survivors that included vulnerable beginnings with dreams shattered, and survival skills learned where play should have been. Torture that made an episode of *Law & Order: Special Victims Unit* seem like a fairy tale. Daily dealing with life and death hanging in the balance as if it were a normal agenda. Tears over what she missed out on: prom, homecoming, turkey around the table at Thanksgiving, or anyone putting her school work on the refrigerator. The simple things that never existed for her and all the things that never should have been.

Story after story piled up. I carried each one.

Dark stories where light broke in and a chance at freedom came. The page turned for her. A new chapter started. Wings of Refuge became her home for a day, a month, a year or two. One more girl got safe and learned to hope again or for the first time. Like the afternoon the Holy Spirit nudged me to let Molly know that in the Wings home, *we have never worked with a prostitute.* She gave me a look like I was a crazy woman. I repeated it. *A prostitute has never lived in this home. You are not a prostitute. Your body was prostituted.* A moan and a weep came out like mine and Joseph's. I held her trembling body while she realized that her *body* was prostituted, but she was not one as the Holy Spirit spoke through me and called out her true identity for her to receive where the stamp *prostitute* had been. A short time later in a coffee shop, she found her voice and spoke truth to a government official as she bravely shared her story and hope in Jesus, *"I am not a prostitute, I am a strong woman loved by God."*

The stories I carried changed me. I saw the world differently because it was so radically different for so many I now knew.

Nora Jane[*]

Nora Jane was born into *the life*. She was the paycheck for her mom to get drugs. Sold by her mom until authorities removed her. Sold inside the foster care system until she ran away and took to the streets. Sold because she was an easy target to be lured in by a pimp who would cash in on her lifetime of vulnerabilities once she was on the streets. She had crossed the line and was barely an adult physically but tired and old in every other way when she went a little rouge and kept a portion of money that was *not hers* from her pimp. Her pimp found out. It was lights out for Nora. She was replaceable. Her pimp tortured her with the goal of death until a moment of sanity hit him and he took her to the hospital. Her safety in the hospital was short lived and he kidnapped her out to finish the job he had started. In the middle of burning her with cigarettes, ripping off her fingernails, and shaving her head he dropped to the ground. Frozen in fear, she thought it was a sick joke. He didn't move. She heard a *"dude's"* voice telling her to leave. She looked around, there was no *"dude"* in the room. She heard the voice tell her again, "*If you don't leave now you will die.*" With adrenaline rushing, she stepped over her pimp and ran outside. A car was stopped at the corner of the street and asked her if she needed help. She said, "*Yes!*" She fled death that day and eventually got life with Jesus. On a car ride together over a year after this maddening night in her life, she cranked up the stereo and we both belted out the lyrics, *"I'm no longer a slave to fear, I am a child of God."*

The stories grew my faith.

---

[*] *The names in any story of a Wings of Refuge participant have been changed to honor the confidentiality of each woman.*

Carla

Carla had many months of safety and success at Wings until a chunk of change came through a back payment from government support. She left Wings without a trace, threw away her *normal* clothes, purchased clothes that made her feel like a prostitute, and paid an Uber to take her to the airport to catch the next flight out. She had money of her own for the first time in a long time and was motivated by the deceiving thought of how many drugs she could buy. For decades she had lived the life of addiction, the streets, and being controlled by pimps. As the airport got closer, the feelings of people who loved her at Wings seemed farther away. She thought about the dog, her friends, her room, and her bed at Wings. On the streets she would have none of that. Her tears let her know she couldn't get on the next flight out. The Uber driver stopped at the curb of the airport. Unable to get out of the car she exclaimed to her driver, "*Lady, you gotta take me back home!*" Her driver replied, "*That is going to be really expensive!*"

It's ok I have a lot of money!" She responded.

Wouldn't you know, shortly after coming back home to Wings, good old Joseph was the main character in morning devotions. She related to his life and saw the full circle healing of her own. "*Yeah it's like the guy who kidnapped me, raped me, and sold me for weeks out of his semi and then dumped me in the middle of Iowa when it was below zero. It was for good, so I could come to Wings and get sober.*"

I carried her story and sometimes her story carried me.

Sara

"Today we are going to do a one-on-one on forgiveness," Sara told me from across the table in what I thought was going to be a fun coffee date before her graduation from Wings. She had a mission. She pulled out a folder with a sheet of bible verses, a devotional reading, and an adult coloring page tucked inside. *WOW! The trauma groups and morning devotions are sticking and paying off*, I thought seeing her organized plan for our morning together. She told me that God wanted her to openly share her story of forgiveness with me. She started with how she forgave her birth parents who abandoned her and ended by sharing that she forgave her pimp who controlled and abused her and murdered one of her friends. Then we read the devotion she had prepared on forgiveness. My assignment was to go home, color the page, and forgive whoever I may need to forgive.

I was stunned. The night before, I had asked my small group to pray for me ... that I would be able to forgive my parents who I was struggling deeply to forgive. Needless to say, I knew what I needed to go home and do. The rest of the coffee date with Sara was a fun blur.

Chapter 17

And So Somehow

> *... and so, somehow, attaining resurrection from the dead.*
>
> —Philippians 3:11 NIV

And so somehow, (Philippians 3:11): it's my favorite part. There is only one way to be connected into a restored relationship with God: receive Jesus—but *and so somehow resurrection* happens in countless ways throughout our lives. It's the way that is made when there seems to be no way. Impossible becomes possible. Forgiveness flows.

The forgiveness I offered myself splashed over. It rippled into forgiving others. For me that came right down to the hardest part, forgiving my parents. I spent time with the Lord forgiving my mom and walked in that forgiveness. It was a process, not a moment—a daily decision to make even though outcomes I hoped for were not happening. I loved her. I wanted her in my life. I went to her numerous times to talk about hard things. It ended up hurting more than helping. I learned that there was one person whose choices and attitude I could control: my own. My counselor encouraged me to see my mom as a broken woman whom God loved and set boundaries in that love. I did. I connected with her on the neutral loving ground of flowers, recipes, and her grandkids.

My father died during the first year Wings of Refuge was open. I wept. There was no happy ending even though the world felt a little safer to me. Years later in an unexpected moment of worship God showed me how he saw my dad and how completely level the ground at the foot of the cross really is. A compelling love for my father filled me. It was not the excruciating thing that I thought it would be to forgive him. The years of overthinking before it was. I forgave him. I let him go. I was free.

The beauty is that **with the Lord**, the harm done to you and the harm you have done doesn't end in suffering. It ends in resurrection. He makes things new—not just the good stuff, but the horrible stuff too. Glory wins out. And when God's glory shows up, everything changes.

The place of brokenness that I thought would take me out became a powerful place to stand on. My pain and problems had me white-knuckling through life and holding onto fear. Jesus said, *Stand up. Take up your cross, and* I did. With Jesus, abuse, violation, and sin do not have the final say: resurrection does. Jesus declares #metoo on the cross but he didn't stay on the cross as a victim. He finished the work and came back to life as Victor.

Do not be conformed any longer to the pattern of this world, be transformed by the renewing of the mind.

—Romans 12:2 AMP

Good news! The mind injured in the pattern of this world can be renewed.

Matt Chandler, in *Recovering Redemption*, shares how he moved to a new house across town. He had to consciously tell himself to turn a different way at the stop light when going home from work after the move. The old way was autopilot, but he didn't live in the old house anymore. One busy day without thinking, he actually drove into the driveway of his old house. As soon as he did, he realized, *You don't live here anymore.* He had to train his brain to think anew. So do we.

Brains can heal. Minds can be new. Lies can be replaced with truth. Shattered and fractured places can be turned into transformed thinking and living. There is life to the full. Love melts our hard hearts. Truth builds us up. Forgiveness frees us. And hope does not ever disappoint. Our God is the Healer and partners with us in our willingness to receive His power to redeem. It's a process. The process is as important as the outcomes it produces. It's a paradox of instant miracles and the slow process of change.

Generational bondage and self-deception in me was replaced with truth. Pathways in my brain healed. At a cellular level I heard Him declare, *Very good*, about me, and I agreed. I didn't just know the truth or hear it from God and others, I sided with it and took hold of it for myself.

I am God's treasure, made in His image: His beloved child. I am lovable and worthy of care. I am His workmanship—His masterpiece, a part of His very good plan. I have a voice that can be used appropriately. I cannot fix people. I do not have to pay for my sins or the sins of others. I can take appropriate responsibility, own my part, and live as a free woman no matter what others do or don't do. I can forgive and be forgiven. I am a human being, not a human doing. I am strong, brave, and capable. When I was a little girl, there were a lot of things that I did not get to decide. I was at the mercy of adults. I am an adult now. I decide. In Jesus Christ I am an overcomer. I am protected by His wings of refuge. I have a very rich and powerful Heavenly Father and I am the apple of His eye. I have dignity and value. My body is a temple where God dwells. Resurrection power, the same power that raised Jesus from the dead, raises dead things in me. I have authority in Jesus Christ. I have been adopted. I belong to Him and with Him. What Jesus gets, I get.

I can walk into a room without anxiety and speak with confidence, unapologetic of who I am because I know who and whose I am. It is a daily process: a lifetime renewal with joy and sorrow, setbacks and success.

And so somehow, resurrection happened in me. I swam in the deep waters of the ocean of God's love. He just kept getting better. I just kept going. The place of my greatest shame became the catalyst for God's glory to flow through me. The place of pain became a place of triumph. I saw His glory in my deepest wound and it dazzled me. The weakness of my abuse is the strength of my calling.

And so somehow resurrection makes me want to shout, *God, you had me at 'hello.' Thank you for loving me every time I ran away from you; thank you for being the Father that stood waiting. You continually weave a gold thread of faith through all of the messy things of my life. You are amazing!*

You showed me and so, somehow, resurrection through the fellowship of suffering and the obedience of taking up my cross allowed me to take my mind off of myself to serve others, and in the process you healed them and me. You pulsed resurrection power through honest friendships, deep community, and me—a lifeless woman.

AND SO SOMEHOW

Resurrection flows continually through your living word: A steady husband, a healing family, and wonderful counselors like you that guide me into resurrection thinking and living. You resurrected my little-girl dream of speaking on a stage and drew me into your Kingdom agenda. You spoke and so, somehow, resurrection and quietly pursued me; your goodness and mercy chased me even when I ran. You ran to me. You are my inheritance, my freedom, my Song! Help me to sing!"

Chapter 18

And They Lived

And they lived happily ever after. I like stories to end this way, don't you? Tidied up and packaged beautifully with a crisp bow on the top. Cinderella marries Prince Charming and dances with both glass slippers on her feet. For years I wished my life was a happily-ever-after social media highlight reel. I love the highlights. I bet you do too. But the incredible raw, real, unfiltered beauty found behind closed doors with little recognition is beyond anything the highlights can offer. Real is full of unknowns, plot twists, and phone calls that change everything.

I sat on mom's hospital bed holding her hand in one of those plot twist moments wondering how we got here. My stepfather had just beaten stage four cancer at 85 years old and *she* was the one receiving hospice care.

Mom had been in and out of hospitals most of my adult life. This was different. She had that faraway look and was somewhere else sorting things out. Mom was dying. It was happening. I was trying to compute.

I sat on one side of her bed as *her joy* with my sister Lori, *her sunshine* on the other. We were three women woven through her lifetime, facing a sad goodbye. There had been decades of ever-so-sweet cherished memories, intermixed with climactic tension in recent years that had seemed to overshadow the good ones, as Mom chose to hang on to what *smile and look* pretty promised by numbing her pain while we learned to let go.

I looked at my sister: the only one who had made me laugh when had I hit the iceberg of heartbreak. How her heart shined like the sun in life's storms was a marvel to me. I noticed we both had a few smile wrinkles from being Mom's joy and sunshine as we sang, prayed, cried, read scriptures to Mom, and deep in our souls wished things could have been different.

Family was notified. Many were coming. Everyone rallied the best they knew how in the midst of the past, a pandemic, and cancer recovery. We were informed that, due to insurance reasons, mom needed to leave the hospital. We lovingly prepared a room for Mom inside our empty-nester home, just like she had for Grandma. In the morning, we would meet the doctor to make final plans for her transport to come and live out her final days in our home.

Morning came. I drove the snowy roads to the hospital. The same song that had played the night before as I had left the hospital parking lot came on again as I drove out of our driveway. Up until last night I had never heard this song. Heaven's truth poured out of my speakers as tears poured out of my ducts, hearing the melody sung of a weary traveler.

No more searching
Heaven's healing's gonna find where all the hurt is
When Jesus calls, we'll lay down all our heavy burdens
Carry on,
Weary traveler, restless soul
You were never meant to walk this road alone
It'll all be worth it so just hold on
Weary traveler, you won't be weary long
—"Weary Traveler" by Jordan St. Cyr[5]

Say the Unsaid

Mom was no longer communicating with words when my sister and I greeted her. At this point the doctor determined she was far enough along in her dying process that insurance would now cover her care to remain in the hospital if we wanted. In the doctor's estimation, Mom only had days left, if that. We asked the doctor what she would do if it was her mom. She said Mom was really looking forward to coming to my home, that it was possible that she may have a final rally to enjoy some moments together, and that the transport would not cause her any more stress or hurt her. She affirmed that it would be ok to stick with the plan, but the decision was up to us. The doctor's words combined with COVID-19 restrictions that made being together in a hospital room difficult and uncomfortable, made Plan A stick. My sis and I talked through last-minute details. Ready to execute the mission, I headed out of Mom's room to drive home and meet the ambulance there.

---

5 St. Cyr, Jordan. "Weary Traveler." This Little Fire / BEC Worship, 2021.

Something inside stopped me. Spirit-led, I floated back around.

"Mom, there's nothing to worry about anymore," I spoke, as I nuzzled up to her ear and held her hand tight. The words tumbled out of me like a prepared script.

"We have everything taken care of. All you have to do is rest and find Jesus. I've had an encounter with The Light of His Glory. It's the most amazing thing you can imagine. There's nothing to be afraid of. You are gonna slip into that Light. It will be amazing! Don't worry; we'll take care of Grandpa. All is forgiven and free. I love you, Mom."

Instant freedom flowed for the residue of things left undone. I kissed her forehead and walked out.

It was the last time I saw my mom alive. Our plan at 10:00 am that morning was to transfer Mom to my house. God's plan at 10:00 am was to transfer her to His.

In a moment, the woven tapestry of Mom's life flipped over and the beautiful masterpiece Jesus weaved with His Glory was revealed. *And so, somehow, resurrection* came to Mom. She was absent from her body and present with the Lord. Free. Complete. Whole.

I walked into Mom's room moments after her death. *Smile and look pretty* was nowhere to be found. Something better had taken its place. Raw beauty in those gathered, openly weeping while holding on to one another—and Jesus.

I looked at Mom's lifeless body. The woman tied to so much here on earth was free. The weary traveler was home. *And so, somehow, resurrection* came to me. I knew people were not angels or demons, heroes or villains; they are people doing the best that they can. Sometimes people's best hurts and breaks us. Other times it blesses, provides, encourages, and makes us.

AND THEY LIVED

What if we dropped the last three words from, *and they lived happily ever after* to read, *and they lived*. Makes more sense, don't you think? Like they lived real blood-sweat–and-tears lives filled with weeping and rejoicing through the high points, low points, and all the regular boring Tuesdays in between.

There was a lot of *and they lived* between my birth and Mom's death: a lot of brokenness and a ton of pain that I don't think either one of us counted on—things that made holding her hand feel strange in those last days. And there was something else: love. Love lived between mom and me as I remembered her encouragement to *rise above it* when life was hard and the small moments of singing *Jesus loves me* and praying *Now I lay me down to sleep* that were incredibly big now.

How did we get here? Suffering for sure, but love so much more. The fuel produced in the collision of suffering and resurrection is love in its finest form. Love is where I began when God knitted me in my mother's womb. My wrestling question of how to honor my father and mother is settled. I honor my father and mother by living out their knitted-together-DNA, called "me," living in God's love and freedom. Love is what brought us here. Love is where I am headed. Love is where Mom went.

Chapter 19

Life Goes On

With the Dutchman

The conflict did eventually end between the steady Dutchman and me. We gave it to God and drove to therapy, waiving our white flags in surrender and calling a truce. We were both right. The kids were hurting and needed help *and* we needed to love each other and be one. Our peace treaty included getting rid of religious thinking and acting, facing our fears in order to stop self-promoting and self-protecting, letting go of judgment and critical spirits and learning how to be gentle parents and spouses who are not passive victims, avoiders, or power controlling dictators. Adjusting out of our own way or the other person's way is grueling work. We learn to adjust to God together by humbling down and standing unoffended in order to truly become loving and forgiving people of peace in Jesus.

We are still compelled to love our neighbor, take the gospel to the ends of the earth, and realize that also includes the one next to us in bed and the ones within our walls.

The best way to change the world is to love God, love yourself, love your spouse, and love your family. Strong people, marriages, and families are what change the world.

—Warren Jacobs

The Holy Spirit freed me from my struggle with being a divorced and remarried woman in the account of the woman at the well (John 4). When Jesus met her at the well, he asked her to go and get her husband. She could only reply, *I have no husband.* He already knew. *You are right when you say you have no husband. The fact is, you have had five husbands, and the man you now have is not your husband.* What a conundrum. She could not go back and reconcile with all five husbands. She could not fix her past. Still, he did not relent in offering her himself: Living Water, because of her history of marriages that had gone south. He simply said, *Drink and you will never be thirsty again.* She drank. It changed her. It changed her so much that she was compelled to run and tell her entire community, (the ones who treated her as an outcast) "Come and meet the man who told me everything I ever did; could this be the Messiah?"

Many in her community were changed because of her testimony.

Her story changed me. Through her testimony I knew I could not go back and fix my past marriage, divorce, and remarriage track record. I could walk in humility and repentance where I am with the life I have and the spouse I have. We could drink living water in spite of the past. Untangle is what our counselor calls it. That is what we do.

And so somehow resurrection wells up in our daily living now even though we are still as different as night and day. When we allow our strengths to unite us—it's magical! We found a covenant love that I did not think was possible. Our marriage is a companionship to help each other heal and head to Heaven. We have to work on it every single day.

And wouldn't you know that it turns out my man had some wounds of his own. He can leave if he needs to leave but I love him. I'm not going anywhere.

With My Kids

My story of suffering and resurrection impacted my boys and stepchildren in the worst and best of ways. Oh how I have wished I could go back with the tools I have now and give their hearts what they needed then. If I could go back I would linger and hold little chubby hands longer, read *just one more* bedtime story without question, and be present to help their hearts navigate the wounds of what they have been through—or prevent them all together. For a long time I would have given everything to go back for a do-over. I had to come to the realization that those little ones are not coming back and there are no do-overs. I said goodbye to those little ones and let them go in my heart. This allowed me to say hello in the present and be present with them not acting out of past regret.

So far I've created two rings out of grandma's three diamonds and wear the titles of mother-in-law, and nana/grandma with delight.

I love my step children as if they were my own flesh and blood and live in the reality that they are not. I am learning to go at their pace instead of mine. I see evidence that the pace is working when my step-daughter freely belts out, "What's wrong with your face?" as my thoughts are worn all over it. With gratitude in my heart I'm thankful she is becoming confident to speak her mind with me. What's wrong with your face has become a natural que that makes us laugh and know it's time to say it out loud, process together, let it go, and move on.

I radically accept reality just the way it is. Our children are on their own journeys of suffering and resurrection now. They have each taught me more about bravery and love than they will ever know.

With Ministry and Mission

There is *one more girl* that I didn't mention whose story I carry. Her name is Bev. She had a dream one night many years before she even knew what Wings of Refuge was. In her dream she died and was in the presence of the Lord. Standing before the Lord she knew he was giving her more time on earth, he told her to *Go and work on your sisters.* She woke up. Her dream was a real encounter with the Lord. She journaled what happened and wrestled with what *work on your sisters meant* for a long time. A friend casually told her about Wings of Refuge. They looked it up online. Lo and behold there was an open position for the executive director. The Lord led Bev to Wings of Refuge where she worked on her sisters with humble servant-hearted leadership that grew the mission. Sometimes I think the sister she worked on the most was me. How many times did I hear her say, *Joy, it's good enough* when my excellence turned the corner into perfection. When you are on this type of mission together I suspect the bond is somewhat similar to the one that forms when you are in the military on the front lines of battle. A sisterhood developed as we ran the little rescue shop that plucked women out of the hell of sex trafficking. Bev completed her mission at Wings of Refuge as the Lord moved through her to grow the organization to a place where he told her it was time for someone else to lead.

In the mix of COVID-19 craziness and a season of serious attacks from the enemy in my personal life and in the ministry, I also stepped away from my formal role at Wings of Refuge. It was gut wrenching. Yet, *and so somehow* resurrection prevailed.

Others carry her story now. God continues to end exploitation for one more girl through a cast of beautifully-made-in-his-image people who fiercely love like Jesus. My calling remains secure and the sisterhood between Bev and me is alive and well.

With Wisdom

Sometimes I wonder, *Why couldn't I have started with the wisdom that took so long to find? I could have used it to raise my sweet boys, love a spouse til death do us part, believe the truth—earlier on in life—about who I am from God's perspective and live fearlessly in that identity.*

When I sit with Wisdom, she tells me, *Accept reality just the way it is; simply be thankful for it all; frame everything through the lens of love and forgiveness, and do the best you can with what you have.* Wisdom allows me to continually let go of fear and come into love. To be turned into love. Wisdom speaks through the hard seasons, *This is not the whole story,* and through the sweet ones, *Soak it up and savor it.*

Wisdom came through the way that it was. Wisdom was being built the whole time like a pristine cathedral constructed over the course of decades, not a prefab-stick-built home put up in a day.

I'm still learning Wisdom's way.

AND SO SOMEHOW

I love this quote.

> *Sometimes, when we lose ourselves in fear and despair, in routine and constancy, in hopelessness and tragedy, we can thank God for Bavarian sugar cookies. And, fortunately, when there aren't any cookies, we can still find reassurance in a familiar hand on our skin, or a kind and loving gesture, or subtle encouragement, or a loving embrace, or an offer of comfort, not to mention hospital gurneys and nose plugs, an uneaten Danish, soft-spoken secrets, and Fender Stratocasters, and maybe the occasional piece of fiction. And we must remember that all these things, the nuances, the anomalies, the subtleties, which we assume only accessorize our days, are effective for a much larger and nobler cause. They are here to save our lives. I know the idea seems strange, but I also know that it just so happens to be true.*
>
> —Zach Helm, *Stranger Than Fiction*[6]

Watermelon on my back deck that was amazingly sweet in the bitter season of truth-telling and pain-feeling was my Bavarian sugar cookie. The simple things are wildly profound. There is a greater glory being worked out for us in *all* things: every second that we live, even when we can't see it. Have faith. He's there.

Just like Joseph, I bless my story. I accept my life for what it is. I don't have it all figured out. It's far from perfect. I journey from

---

6 Forster, Marc. 2006. Stranger Than Fiction. United States: Columbia Pictures.

glory to glory and strength to strength. Sometimes the more I understand, the more questions I have. The more intimate my affection grows into the perfection of Christ, the clearer I see my human imperfections. I previewed a taste of Heaven on earth when my suffering collided with God's light. I get glimpses, samples, and tastes here on earth as his Kingdom comes within me. Some things will remain dim until Heaven and there will be a day when I will live forever in that Glorious Light of who He is, just like Mom and Grandma do, and the last three words can be added to read, *and she lived happily ever after.*

Chapter 20

Dancing Again

Tonight would close out a year of over 60 speaking events. I shared the mission of Wings of Refuge like usual and what it was going to take to renovate and open a larger home for many more girls. The night ended. A large stack of names of people with skills and abilities was compiled that proved God would accomplish this. I rested in that and went to Florida to get away and write for a few days.

In the quiet slow-down of being alone, the Lord showed me what I had overlooked in the long journey through the short sentences of Philippians 3:10,11.

> *I want to know Christ and the power of his resurrection, to share in the fellowship of his suffering, becoming like him in his death, and so, somehow, to attain resurrection from the dead.*
>
> —Philippians 3:10,11 NIV

I jumped from suffering to resurrection every time. Just like I glossed over God as Judge in the old testament, I scooted right past *becoming like him in his death*.

Death needed to happen. I knew it. Victim-me had to go for good. Once and for all. God lovingly cared for me as a victim. He walked me out of so much. I was not a victim anymore. No part of it was helpful to a future of thriving. Open journal and open heart was the routine as I lay on the floor and penned it out. I let go of the victim I once was and gave her to Jesus. As I did, he gave her back. It was my "ashes to beauty" moment: the one I had been waiting for.

You are not a dead victim. You are a King's daughter and my victorious child. Live.

Life is still a far cry from perfect but I found Joy, every single part of her through my Philippians 3:10,11 journey of *and so somehow resurrection*. All of me is at the table. I'm not waiting for the ball to drop or constantly zoning out, dissociated and unable to deal with hard things in the present. I know that in every worst-case-scenario, Jesus is there; I am not alone, and I am showing up right along with Him.

Healing Waters

"Will you come out with me? The water is warm, come on!" My husband pleaded.

He had heard a decline to this question on more than one occasion. I was surprised he still asked. I thought about saying, *Who will watch our stuff?* as I sat on my beach towel, instead I said. "Okay."

We inched our way into the crashing ocean waves. They resembled the ones that swept me under as a child. Our bodies swayed to and fro. I squealed with delight, squeezed his hand tight, and realized I had forgotten about *safe*. We jumped wave after wave as they came towards us. I knew deep in my soul:

It's never too late. There is no wasted time with the Lord.

Inside the crashing waves, I found little me, the innocent dandelion dancing girl within. We chatted.

You are so on to something, baby girl. I am so proud of you. Those flowers are so pretty. They make God smile and they make me smile too. You are darling. The songs in your sweet soul are beautiful. They will get lost for a while, but it's ok; you will find them again. I know the waves are scary; they almost take us out. But we learn how to rise above them and make our way to the surface with Jesus. He's not as far away as you think. It's okay to play and splash in the waves. It's okay to squeal and laugh. I'm here. We will laugh and play together. We can be silly and goofy and not think about hard things. Will you come?

You're here! You're here! I'm not alone! she squeals delightfully back into my soul.

Will you teach me to swim? Will you splash with me and hold my hand?

Absolutely! You are a precious little girl. Anyone would be blessed to take hold of your hand. It's a beautiful day. The waves are calling. Let's go!

The Light of Your Glory brings me to Joy. What a *joy* she is. She's dandelion-dancing again.

Afterword

And So Somehow: A Practical Guide

They triumphed over him (the devil) by the blood of the Lamb and the word of their testimony. They did not love their life so much as to shrink from death.

—Revelation 12:11 NIV

I know this to be true. I overcome through the blood of Jesus and by sharing the words of my testimony. You overcome by reading it. I wrote my story for one reason: To be a witness of Jesus Christ and testify of his Great Love that will never let go. I pray that every word reveals who Jesus Christ is to your precious heart.

It is easy to compare journeys. Many of you may have lives that make mine look like a piece of cake or vice versa. When I first began serving survivors at Wings of Refuge there was a particular day that comparing the lives of two polar opposite stories collided. On a fall afternoon I sat for hours and bore witness to *Cindy's* story that made my brain discombobulate. Taken at an early age: a story that involved repetitive evil over and over to her little body: minimal schooling. No learning to play sports. Just evil. Guns. Blood. Drugs and cockroaches were the props in her childhood. She was sold to the rich and famous, "dope fiends" and everyone in between even before she was in double digits. She had children and lost them while in this hideous life. My heart and brain felt like a ton of the saddest bricks had been dumped in them as I listened. They tell you to be strong enough to handle her pain. I wasn't that day. I left the little Wings home and got in my car numb. I felt out of body. Nothing in life felt normal. Then my phone lit up with a familiar name. I couldn't answer fast enough. It was a friend asking for prayer for her daughter. She had had a rough day at school: while giving a presentation on preparing soup in her class, she spilled the soup.

Worlds collided. I was angry. Seriously? Spilled soup!

I mustered my way through the conversation. To this day I could not tell you how the conversation ended. I went home and poured the held back tears and anger of the afternoon on Jesus and received from him.

He set the record straight.

What a blessing that one has been loved so well that her bottom is spilled soup. Each one has a bottom in life. From spilled soup to a life of violence and extreme abuse. Your bottom is your bottom. No worse. No better. Different? Yes. I died and bled for each one. I resurrected for it all. It all matters to me.

What about you? What is your bottom? Do you know Jesus who died and resurrected for you? Has the light of God collided into what has hurt you most? What is your Joseph weep? Have you forgiven yourself for what you have done or others for what has been done to you? Do you need to get your mind off of your-

AND SO SOMEHOW: A PRACTICAL GUIDE

self and do something nice for someone else? If so, it might just change your life. You can't change the past. You can be set free from it with truth in the present. You can't rewrite your story; you can finish stronger. *And so somehow* makes it possible. Are you on that *and so somehow* road to resurrection? Keep Going! Do you see the fork in the road? Do you need to get off the path of the enemy lying, stealing and destroying your life? Open your heart; let God in. Receive. He loves you. Jesus wants to serve you. You are so incredibly worth it to him.

How will you finish? What will your story tell others? It is my great hope that through these pages something resonated with you and your story and led you to encounter the Spirit of the Lord pursuing you for the first time or in a deeper way.

This book was meant to give you a picture of how God heals wounds, lies, and shame in us, His precious and dearly loved children. Please know there was a whole lot of folding laundry, grocery shopping, bill paying, sleeping, showering, cooking, cleaning, lying on the couch, bleacher butt, laughing out loud with joy, losing my patience and feeling defeat, filling the gas tank of my car, and really regular stuff within all of this. Miracles happen in an instant: soul healing takes time, work, and intention. Often, through my season of deep healing, nothing would seem different, and then a situation would happen and I would notice *Oh my goodness fear isn't holding me hostage: It's gone. Oh my word, my brain is not going to the worst case scenario!* It's like a little freedom party in my soul each time I experience victory.

Live your life and don't forget your heart in the process. It's worth caring for. Heart work is worth the work. It can make all the regular days better.

For some of you my story may have been hard to read between the lines of what was happening. If you are a logical, practical thinker like my steady Dutchman, here are concrete steps to living a life of "And So Somehow" resurrection.

Practical Ways to Live in "And So Somehow" Resurrection:

1. **Be Still**
   - Center down into quietness—away from schedules, people, screens, and the temptation to scroll social media feeds.
   - Get a journal. Open it up. Write your fears, struggles, stresses.
   - Write anything that you carry in your heart: the good, bad, or boring.
   - Sometimes writing letters to yourself or others that you do not intend to send can be helpful.
   - Pour it all out on Jesus and LISTEN to what he has to say. He is the God who speaks.

2. **Go to God**
   - Spend time with the Lord in His word. It is a Living Word that can speak to you intimately through the power and presence of the Holy Spirit in you. It's great to listen to someone else teach the Bible and share what God has revealed to them through it, and you also need to take it in for yourself. Ask the Holy Spirit to lead you. He will.
   - Pray. Talk to God about anything. All the time. Anywhere. Out loud. Silently. Alone and with others. Prayer is powerful! Prayer is speaking and listening to what God wants to say to you personally.

3. **Drive to Therapy**
   - Find a trusted counselor who is filled with the Holy Spirit and depends on God's word (and also fits your particular need and your personality).
   - Give it time and go regularly.
   - Go until they put you on the *call as needed* list.

4. **Feel Your Feelings**
   - Feelings are for feeling, not for fixing. Feelings are God-given, and God is an emotional God. It's okay to feel. Feelings are not right or wrong, they just are. They are not to be avoided, pushed down, ignored, reacted upon, or lived out of. Feelings are not meant to guide your life. They are thoughts generated from sensations–known as emotions–in our bodies. Feeling your feelings, rather than reacting upon them, helps you to become emotionally mature.

5. **Forgive**
   - There is so much to learn about forgiveness. I could write an entire book about it. There are many who have done just that. If you are struggling, find books on forgiveness to understand what it is and what it is not. Some can forgive quickly. Some hurts are easier to forgive than others. Forgiveness is a decision and a lifestyle. Forgiveness is the oxygen of the Kingdom. We forgive because we have been forgiven. God cut off the effects of what we did and what was done to us on the cross through Jesus. Forgiveness frees you in deep places! It's radical.

6. **Utilize Healing Tools**
    - The following are strategic and radical tools the Lord brought into my life to aid in healing wounds from my past. I highly recommend each one!
        - The Ultimate Journey - www.theultimatejourney.org
        - Living Fearless/ Jamie Winship - identityexchange.com
        - Anesis Retreats - anesisretreats.com
        - Emotionally Healthy Spirituality - www.emotionallyhealthy.org
        - Blessing Your Spirit by Arthur Burk and Sylvia Gunter
        - Soul Care by Dr. Rob Reimer

7. **Connect in Community**
    - It is said we become like the top-five people we hang out with. Who is that in your life? Are they bringing you up or down?
    - Ask the Holy Spirit to provide a community of authentic people who receive from and follow Jesus and are filled with His Spirit. Pursue the power and presence of God together in intimate community. This could be in family, a few friends, church, Bible study, or a small group gathering (the real and raw kind). Remember: There are no perfect people and church hurt is real. I've received it. I've done it. It's still worth it. We need each other. Be in community and grow in Jesus together. We are not meant to do life alone (not even introverts).

8. **Be Gentle**
   - Compassion and empathy are great friends of healing. Start with you. Let the Holy Spirit love you and learn how to be kind and compassionate to yourself. If you want to be able to love your neighbor you must first love yourself (*love your neighbor as yourself*) not the world's selfish love: the agreement with God and what he thinks love which cannot hold a candle to any kind of human or worldly love. Affirm yourself; side with God on what he says is true about you. Over time, it will begin to flow out of you and into others naturally.

9. **Play**
   - Find hobbies or activities that make you come alive. Forget about hard stuff. For me that is spending time with family and friends, walking, biking, paddle boarding, kayaking, playing games, traveling, interior design, and decorating.
   - Laugh! I'm not typically a funny person so I hang out with others who are. It's great medicine for the soul!

10. **Make Your Bed**
    - Establish rhythms: simple routines.
    - If you have lived in survival mode, building routines can help you find stability.
    - Structure can offer security, but be flexible and willing to pivot. If you tend to lean towards perfectionism, you might try not making your bed every now and then. ☺

11. Rest
- Life has a never-ending to-do list. Learn how to truly rest. Take a sabbath day, a sabbatical time away when possible. Take a nap. I regularly take a 15–20 power nap. It is a game changer. Sometimes sleep is what we need when life is really unsettled. A rested mind and body can help us see things from a different perspective!
- Learn the power of pausing for a minute, an hour, a day, a week, a month, or a year.
- Live in a state of rest—you can be a resting powerhouse with God and do more in this place than you ever thought possible!

12. Learn
- Be a lifelong student. Let wisdom teach you. There are many Christ-centered, Spirit-led books, podcasts, videos, and websites. Start digging into them: listen while you work out, drive, or cook dinner!
- Learn something new. Take a good risk. Accomplish a goal or a dream one step at a time! You can do it!
- Have others who are mentoring you with wisdom from their walk with Jesus, their encounters with the Holy Spirit, and their insight from the Word.

13. Move
- I was not an athlete in high school. I started randomly running when I was separated from my first husband. I gradually progressed from a block to 12 miles. Trust me: If I can do this, so can you! It was a saving grace. I did not know it then, but the coined "happy hormone" known as serotonin is released when you work out. It wards off depressive and anxious feelings of dread. Isn't it

magnificent how God made our bodies?! Find an activity that fits and go for it. It doesn't always have to be formal exercise: trim trees in your yard; deep-clean your house, or clean out your garage. (Check with a physician for health concerns before beginning.)
- I love this resource: Revelation Wellness www.revelationwellness.org

14. Listen to Music
- When you sing it does so many magnificently cool things inside your brain. Your amygdala (the part of our brain that regulates emotions and encodes memories) actually dances! Worship is warfare: Satan cannot be where the worship of the Lord is! Turn up the tunes! Sing your heart out! It changes the atmosphere.

15. Choose Gratitude
- Grandpa Bob's cancer came back. When he was told there would be no more treatment and was being discharged from the hospital to go home and die, his response without hesitation was, "The Lord told me he would be with me until the end of the age. What do I have to worry about? I have lived a good life; I have a great welcoming committee in Heaven; I will miss you kids, but I'm ready to go home." He was one of the most gratitude-filled people I have ever met. His attitude did not flinch. It stayed steady and thankful until he went to live in Heaven.
- Develop an attitude of gratitude. I know it's a cheesy cliche phrase but it is also true. What works for you? Wake up and thank God for three things before your feet hit the floor; have a list of gratitude; start a gratitude

journal; go on a gratitude walk. Sometimes my husband and I just ask this simple question over dinner: What was the best part of your day (gratitude)?
- I spoke to Bev—you know the one who worked hard on this sister —recently, she shared her little grandson's prayer. *Thank you Jesus for my hamburger, the cheese and my pickle!* Have a life of being thankful even for pickles—see what happens when you do!
- Look up. Think about what is true, noble, just, excellent, and praiseworthy—especially on the hard days. Reframe things through the lens of love, i.e., when it's hard instead of *this sucks; I can't; this isn't fair; the world is against me; why does everyone else have things go right except me?* think: *I am gaining perseverance; I am learning and growing; the Lord is carrying me through a storm: my trust in Him is strengthening; I choose faith and belief in Jesus even when I don't see.*

16. Serve Others
- You can serve others by going on a full-blown overseas mission trip. Or you can serve others with simpler things, like a handwritten note, letter in the mail, call, text, meal, surprise gift, or an hour of your time. Give a family member, friend, acquaintance, or even a stranger permission to share their heart while you listen with all of yours. Generosity will take you farther on your healing journey than you thought possible! Do to others what you would want done to you if you were in their situation. It's a game changer for you and them! Double abundant blessings flow!
- If you have a passion to give to or serve survivors of sex trafficking, please reach out to the staff who continue to

carry the mission of Wings of Refuge forward. Wings of Refuge is a Christ-centered organization that provides opportunities for healing and restoration to survivors of sex trafficking and sexual exploitation.
> Website: www.wingsofrefuge.net
> Email: info@wingsofrefugeia.net
> Facebook: facebook.com/wingsofrefuge.ia
> Address: PO Box 2455, Ames, IA 50010

- Mentor someone who needs your story and wisdom in their life. Raise young ones to experience *and so somehow in their lives!*
- Leave your place of heartbreak and pain. Move forward. Share this great love that will never let go to the one in front of you, next to you in bed, or across the world. Here are two places that offer mission trips. One of them is where I met Zoe and everything changed!
    > Robins Nest Children's Home - www.robinsnestchildrenshome.org
    > GoServ Global - goservglobal.org

17. Find Help

- If you are struggling deeply with life-controlling issues, there is help and hope. Here are two places you can turn to right now.
    > Adult and Teen Challenge - www.globaltc.org
    > Celebrate Recovery - www.celebraterecovery.com

About the Author

From the time Joy was little, she dreamed of speaking on a stage. The lies that she came to believe made that dream seem impossible, until the light of God broke through. Joy saw God's glory in her deepest wound; it dazzled her and allowed her to discover her true identity. She co-founded Wings of Refuge, a ministry for women recovering from sex trafficking. Joy was named Outstanding Woman in Corrections by the Iowa Corrections Association and received the Anti-Trafficking Service Award from Governor Kim Reynolds. Today Joy is a passion-filled visionary with a bold testimony of *And So Somehow* resurrection to encourage and mobilize others to receive their God-given identity. When she is not speaking, you can find her at home on Little Wall Lake in Jewell, Iowa, with her husband, Aaron, and their dog, Finn. Joy's greatest joy is Jesus. She is an empty nester who loves family, relationships, coffee, traveling, and interior design.

Invite Joy to Speak!

Joy Fopma
Website: www.joyfopma.com
Phone: 515-776-8680
Email: joyfopma@gmail.com
Facebook: www.facebook.com/joy.fopma

Made in the USA
Monee, IL
15 May 2024